Crocheted Scarves
and Cowls

Crocheted Scarves
and Cowls

35 colourful and contemporary crochet patterns

Nicki Trench

CICO BOOKS

LONDON NEW YORK

Published in 2016 by CICO Books
An imprint of Ryland Peters & Small Ltd
20–21 Jockey's Fields
London WC1R 4BW

www.rylandpeters.com

10 9 8 7 6 5 4 3 2 1

A CIP catalogue record for this book is available from the
British Library.

UK ISBN: 978-1-78249-364-8

Printed in China

Editor: Marie Clayton
Pattern checker: Jane Czaja
Designer: Vicky Rankin
Photographer: Terry Benson
Illustrator: Stephen Dew
Stylist: Rob Merrett

In-house editor: Anna Galkina
Art director: Sally Powell
Production manager: Gordana Simakovic
Publishing manager: Penny Craig
Publisher: Cindy Richards

Contents

Introduction

When I was first commissioned to design 35 crocheted scarves I found it extremely daunting and I had no idea how the overall book was going to look. So I set about taking my time designing each scarf one by one – and the variation in patterns, textures and designs slowly evolved into a wonderful mix and range of techniques, thicknesses and styles. I'm really delighted with the outcome of this book and I think there is a scarf (or three or four!) in here for all ages, styles and levels.

I've spent a considerable amount of time researching scarves to find out what colours and trends are in fashion, so here you'll find glorious chunky scarves, cute pompoms and elaborate edgings. There is a mix of plain and simple styles for beginners and more complex patterns for the seasoned crocheter. Each pattern is graded into four skill levels, if you are more experienced, you'll still love some of the designs for beginners – sometimes simple is best, but if you're up for a challenge the Level 4 designs will be really rewarding to make.

The yarns I've used are all my favourites: Debbie Bliss, Fyberspates and Louisa Harding. These yarn brands are fantastic at bringing out current and fashionable shades as well as a good range of the classics. I've chosen only the softest yarns, because who wants itchy crocheted fabric around the neck? But if you do decide to replace the suggested yarns with your own choice, make sure that you do a tension square to achieve the size given.

Many of the designs were thought up and influenced by my surroundings, near the sea where I live in East Sussex, UK, so the names of the patterns are seaside inspired. If you're taking a walk along a coastline, particularly in the UK, you'll definitely need to wrap up with one of the scarves from this book!

I've really enjoyed making and designing these scarves for you, and I'm sure you're going to love crocheting them as much as you will love wearing them. Enjoy.

basic
techniques

crochet techniques

Crochet has only a few basic stitches and once you've mastered these all extended stitches follow the same principles. Practise the basic stitches before attempting your first pattern. Crochet is easy to undo because you only have one loop on the hook so you can't really go wrong. When practising keep the loops loose – you can work on creating an even tension across the fabric later.

Holding your hook and yarn

Holding the yarn and hook correctly is a very important part of crochet and once you have practised this it will help you to create your stitches at an even tension.

Holding your hook

There are two basic ways of holding the hook. I always teach the pen position as I find this more comfortable. It gives you a more relaxed arm and shoulder.

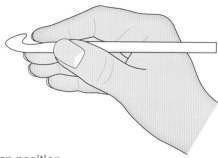

Pen position

Pick up your hook as though you are picking up a pen or pencil. Keeping the hook held loosely between your fingers and thumb, turn the hook so that the tip is facing up and the hook is balanced in your hand and resting in the space between your index finger and your thumb.

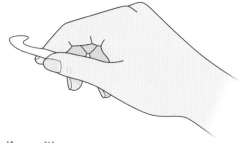

Knife position

But if I'm using a very large hook and chunky yarn, then I may sometimes change and use the knife position. I crochet a lot and I've learned that it's important to take care not to damage your arm or shoulder by being too tense. Make sure you're always relaxed when crocheting and take breaks.

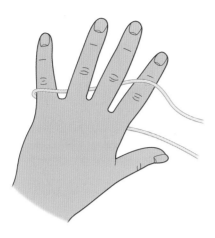

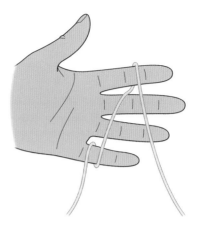

Holding your yarn

Pick up the yarn with your little finger on the opposite hand to the hook, with palm facing towards you, the short end in front of the finger and the yarn in the crease between little finger and ring finger. Turn your hand to face downward (see left), placing the long yarn strand on top of your index finger, under the other two fingers and wrapped right around the little finger. Then turn your hand to face you (see above), ready to hold the work in your middle finger and thumb.

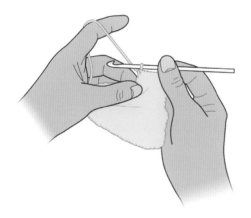

Holding hook and yarn while crocheting

Keep your index finger, with the yarn draped over it, at a slight curve, and hold your work (or the slip knot) using the same hand, between your middle finger and your thumb and just below the crochet hook and loop/s on the hook.

As you draw the loop through the hook, release the yarn on the index finger to allow the loop to stay loose on the hook. If you tense your index finger, the yarn will become too tight and pull the loop on the hook too tight for you to draw the yarn through.

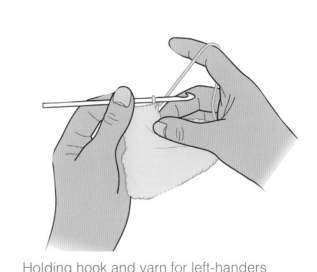

Holding hook and yarn for left-handers

Some left-handers learn to crochet like right-handers, but others learn with everything reversed – with the hook in the left hand and the yarn in the right.

Slip knot

A slip knot is the loop that you put onto the hook to start any stitch in crochet.

1 Make a circle of yarn as shown.

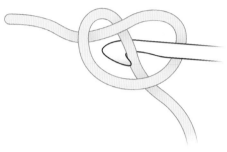

2 In one hand hold the circle at the top where the yarn crosses, and let the tail drop down at the back so that it falls across the centre of the loop. With your free hand or the tip of a crochet hook, pull a loop through the circle.

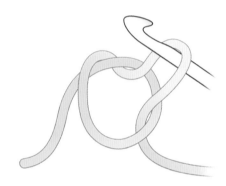

3 This forms a very loose loop on the hook.

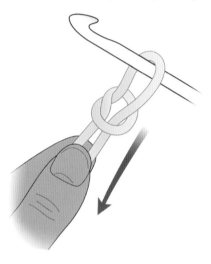

4 Pull both yarn ends gently to tighten the loop around the crochet hook shank.

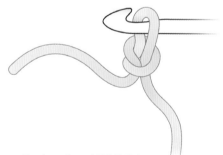

5 Make sure the loop is not TOO tight. It needs to slip easily along the shank.

Chain stitches (ch)

Chains are the basis of all crochet. This is the stitch you have to practise first because you need to make a length of chains to be able to make the first row or round of any other stitch. Practising these will also give you the chance to get used to holding the hook and the yarn correctly.

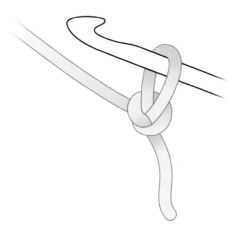

1 Start with the tip of the hook pointed upwards, with the slip knot on your hook sitting loosely so there is enough gap to pull a strand of yarn through the loop on the hook.

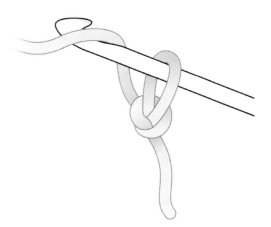

2 Catch the yarn with the hook, circling it around the strand of yarn.

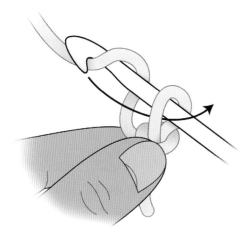

3 As you catch the yarn, turn the tip of the hook downwards, holding the knot immediately under the loop on the hook with your left hand between finger and thumb.

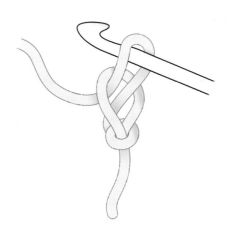

4 Then gently pull the strand of yarn through the loop on the hook. As soon as the tip of the hook comes through the loop, turn the tip of the hook immediately upwards.

Slip stitch (ss)

A slip stitch is the shortest crochet stitch and is usually worked into other stitches rather than into a foundation chain, because it is rarely used to make a whole piece of crochet. It is mainly used to join rounds or to take the yarn neatly along the tops of stitches to get to a certain point without having to fasten off. It can also be used as a joining stitch.

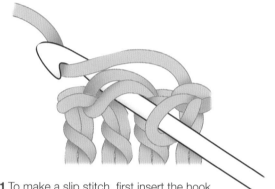

1 To make a slip stitch, first insert the hook through the stitch (chain or chain space). Then wrap the yarn round the hook.

2 Pull the yarn through both the stitch (chain or chain space) and the loop on the hook at the same time, so you will be left with one loop on the hook.

Double crochet (dc)

Double crochet is the most commonly used stitch of all. It makes a firm tight crochet fabric. If you are just starting out, it is the best stitch to start with because it is the easiest to make.

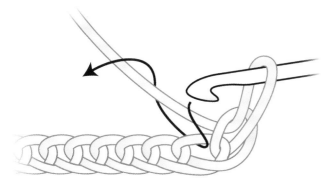

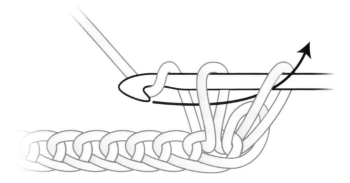

1 Make a foundation chain, then insert the tip of the hook into the 2nd chain from the hook. Catch the yarn with the hook by taking the hook around the back of the yarn strand. Pull the yarn through the chain only with the hook pointed downwards. As soon as you have brought the yarn through, immediately turn the hook upwards – this will help to keep the loop on the hook and prevent it sliding off. Keep the hook in a horizontal position.

2 You will now have two loops on the hook. Wrap the yarn round the hook again (with the hook sitting at the front of the yarn), turn the hook to face downwards and pull the yarn through the two loops, turning the hook to point upwards as soon as you have pulled the yarn through.

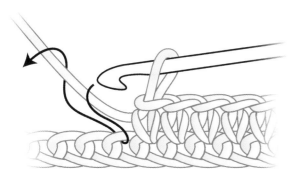

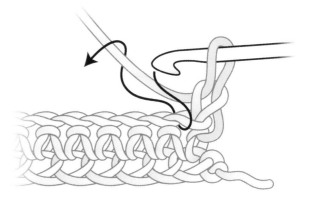

3 One loop is now left on the hook. Keep the hook pointed upwards (this is the default position of the hook until you start the next stitch). Continue working one double crochet into each chain to the end of the foundation chain.

4 Then turn the work to begin the next row. Make one chain and work the first double crochet into the top of the first double crochet in the row below (picking up the two loops at the top of the stitch). Work one double crochet into each double crochet stitch in the row below, to the end of the row.

5 For all subsequent rows, repeat Step 4.

Half treble (htr)

Half trebles are stitches that are the next height up to a double crochet stitch. The yarn is wrapped round the hook first before going into the stitch (or space) and then once pulled through the stitch (or space) there will be three loops on the hook. The middle loop is from the strand that was wrapped round the hook. Before you attempt to pull the yarn through all three stitches, make sure the loops sit straight and loosely on the hook so that you can pull another strand through to complete the stitch.

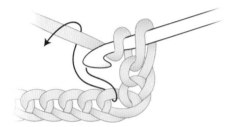

1 Make your foundation chain as usual to start. Before inserting the hook into the work, wrap the yarn round the hook. Then with the yarn wrapped round the hook, insert the hook through the 3rd chain from the hook. Work 'yarn round hook' again (as shown by the arrow).

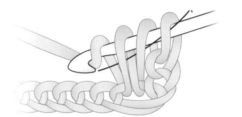

2 Pull the yarn through the chain. You now have three loops on the hook. Yarn round hook again and pull it through all three loops on the hook.

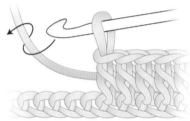

3 You will be left with one loop on the hook. Continue working one half treble into each chain to the end of the foundation chain.

4 Then turn the work to begin the next row. Make two chains. Work one half treble into each half treble stitch in the row below to the end of the row.

5 For all subsequent rows, repeat Step 4.

Treble (tr)

A treble is a very common stitch; it gives a more open fabric than a double crochet or a half treble, which both give a denser fabric, and it's a one step taller stitch than a half treble. As with the half treble, the yarn is wrapped round the hook first before going into the stitch (or space) and then once pulled through the stitch to have three loops on the hook. The middle loop is from the strand that was wrapped round the hook. Before you attempt to pull the yarn through the next two stitches on the hook, make sure the loops sit straight and loosely on the hook so that you can pull another strand through the loops on the hook.

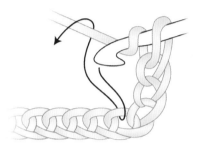

1 Before inserting the hook into the work, wrap the yarn round the hook. Then with the yarn wrapped round the hook, insert the hook through the 4th chain from the hook. Work 'yarn round hook' again (as shown by the arrow).

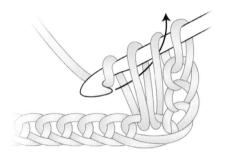

2 Pull the yarn through the chain. You now have three loops on the hook. Yarn round hook again and pull it through the first two loops on the hook.

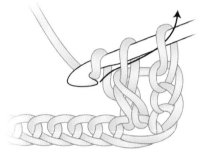

3 You now have two loops on the hook. Yarn round hook again and pull it through the two remaining loops.

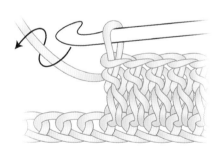

4 You will be left with one loop on the hook. Continue working one treble into each chain to the end of the foundation chain.

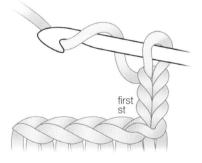

first st

5 Then turn the work to begin the next row. Make three chains. Work one treble into each treble stitch in the row below to the end of the row.

6 For all subsequent rows, repeat Step 5.

Double treble (dtr)

Yarn round hook twice, insert hook into the stitch, yarn round hook, pull a loop through (four loops on hook), yarn round hook, pull the yarn through two stitches (three loops on hook), yarn round hook, pull a loop through the next two stitches (two loops on hook), yarn round hook, pull a loop through the last two stitches.

Increasing

You can increase by working two or three stitches into one stitch or space from the previous row. The illustration shows a two-stitch increase being made in treble.

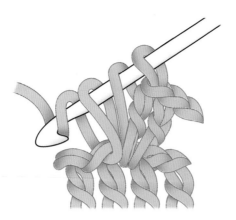

Decreasing

You can decrease by missing the next stitch and continuing to crochet, or by crocheting two or more stitches together. The basic technique for crocheting stitches together is the same for all stitches.

DOUBLE CROCHET TWO STITCHES TOGETHER (dc2tog)

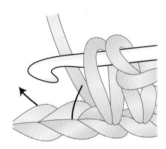

1 Insert the hook into the work, yarn round hook and pull through the work (two loops on hook), insert the hook in the next stitch, yarn round hook and pull the yarn through.

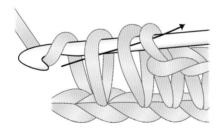

2 Yarn round hook again and pull through all three loops on the hook. You will then have one loop on the hook.

DOUBLE CROCHET THREE STITCHES TOGETHER (dc3tog)

This stitch is a decrease that takes three stitches down into one stitch.

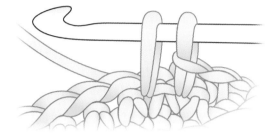

1 Insert the hook in the stitch, yarn round hook, pull the yarn through the work (2 loops on hook).

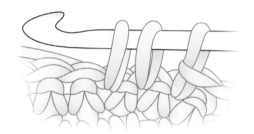

2 Insert the hook in the next stitch, yarn round hook, pull the yarn through the work (3 loops on hook).

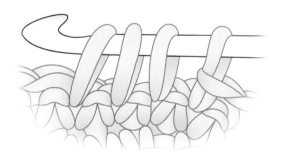

3 Insert the hook in the next stitch, yarn round hook, pull the yarn though the work (4 loops on hook).

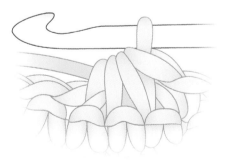

4 Yarn round hook, pull the yarn through all 4 loops on the hook (1 loop on hook). One double crochet three stitches together made.

TREBLE CROCHET THREE STITCHES TOGETHER (tr3tog)

This stitch is a decrease that takes three treble stitches down into one stitch.

1 Yarn round hook, insert the hook in the next stitch (first of the three stitches), yarn round hook, pull the yarn through the work (3 loops on hook).

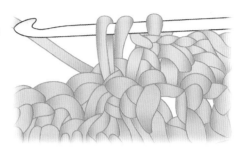

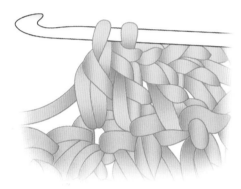

2 Yarn round hook, pull the yarn through the first two loops on the hook (2 loops on hook).

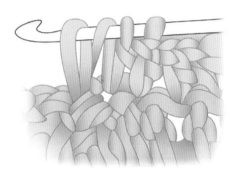

3 Yarn round hook, insert the hook in the next st (second of the three stitches), yarn round hook, pull the yarn through the work (4 loops on hook).

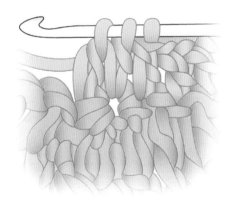

4 Yarn round hook, pull the yarn through the first two loops on the hook (3 loops on hook).

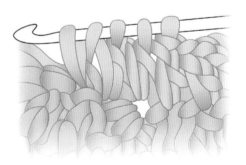

5 Yarn round hook, insert the hook in the next st (third of the three stitches), yarn round hook, pull the yarn through the work (5 loops on hook).

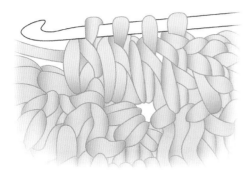

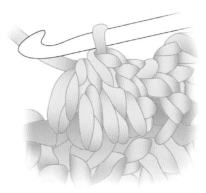

6 Yarn round hook, pull the yarn through the first two loops on the hook (4 loops on hook).

7 Yarn round hook, pull the yarn through all 4 loops on the hook (1 loop on hook).

Three-treble cluster (3trCL)

This cluster is made up of three trebles.

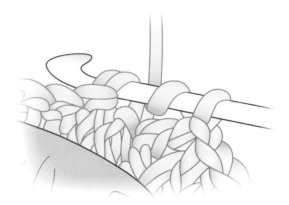

1 Yarn round hook, insert the hook in the stitch (or space).

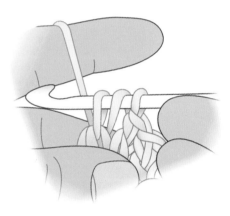

2 Yarn round hook, pull the yarn through the work (3 loops on hook).

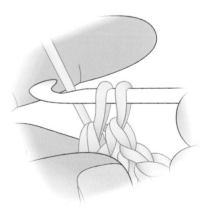

3 Yarn round hook, pull the yarn through 2 loops on the hook (2 loops on hook).

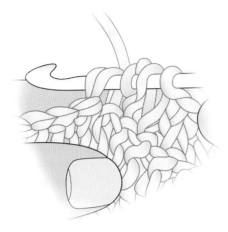

4 Yarn round hook, insert the hook in the same stitch (or space).

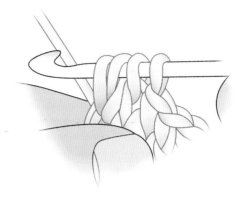

5 Yarn round hook, pull the yarn through the work (4 loops on hook).

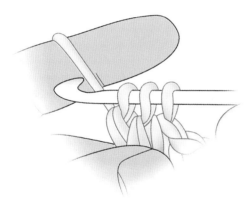

6 Yarn round hook, pull the yarn through 2 loops on the hook (3 loops on hook).

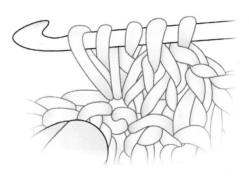

7 Yarn round hook, insert the hook in the same stitch (or space), yarn round hook, pull the yarn through the work (5 loops on hook).

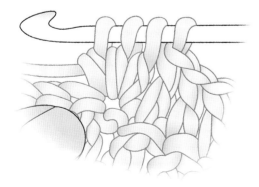

8 Yarn round hook, pull the yarn through 2 loops on the hook (4 loops on hook).

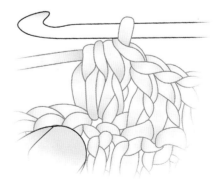

9 Yarn round hook, pull the yarn through all 4 loops on the hook (1 loop on hook). One three-treble cluster made.

Raised treble round front (tr/rf)

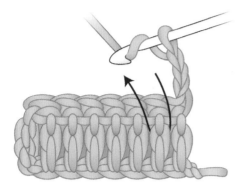

1 Yarn round hook and insert the hook from the front and around the post (the stem) of the next treble from right to left.

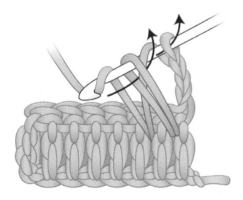

2 Yarn round hook and pull the yarn through the work, yarn round hook and pull the yarn through the first 2 loops on the hook.

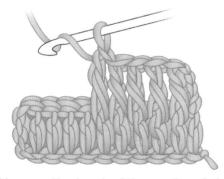

3 Yarn round hook and pull the yarn through the 2 loops on the hook (1 loop on hook). One raised treble round front completed.

beading

Threading beads onto yarn

All the beads must be threaded onto the yarn before you start crocheting. If you run out of beads and need to add more, you will need to cut the yarn at the end of the row/round and thread more beads onto the ball and then join in the yarn again to continue. The size of the hole in the bead is usually too small for a yarn sewing needle eye to go through, and the yarn is too thick to be threaded onto a normal sewing needle, so here is a technique to thread the beads onto the yarn.

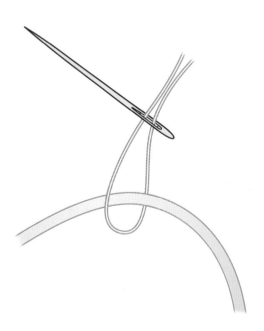

1 Make a loop with some cotton sewing thread and thread a sewing needle with the loop (not the end). Leave the loop hanging approx 2.5cm (1in) from the eye of the needle. Pull the yarn end through the loop of the thread.

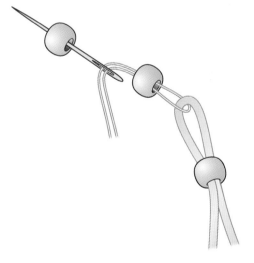

2 Thread the beads (two or three at a time), onto the sewing needle, pushing them down onto the strand of the yarn. Continue to thread beads until the required number is reached.

Beads can be placed when working with the wrong or the right side of the work facing you. The beads will always sit on the front (right side) of the work.

Placing a bead on the wrong side of the work when working in trebles

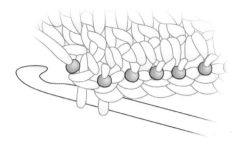

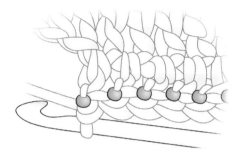

1 Yarn round hook, insert the hook into the stitch, yarn round hook, pull the yarn through the stitch (3 loops on hook), yarn round hook, pull the yarn through the first 2 loops on the hook (2 loops on hook). Slide the bead up the yarn strand and place it close to the back of the work.

2 Yarn round hook, pull the yarn through both loops on the hook. The bead is now placed at the back of the work.

Placing a bead on the right side of the work when working in trebles

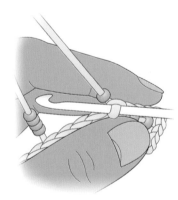

1 Slide bead up yarn at the back of the work to sit close to the hook.

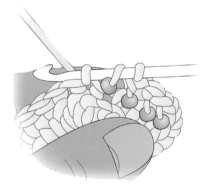

2 Yarn round hook, insert hook in st, yarn round hook, pull yarn through stitch. Slide bead over the hook from the back to the front so that it sits at the front of the work. Complete treble in normal way.

tassels, fringes and pompoms

Tassels and fringes

Tassels are single clusters of knotted yarn ends; if they are repeated close together along an edge this creates a fringe.

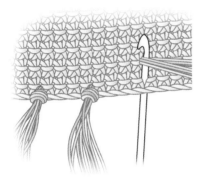

1 Cut strands of yarn to the length given in the pattern. Take one or more strands and fold in half. With the right side of the project facing, insert a crochet hook in one of the edge stitches from the wrong side. Catch the bunch of strands with the hook at the fold point.

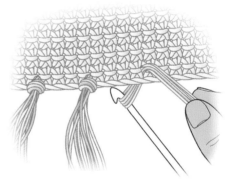

2 Draw all the loops through the stitch.

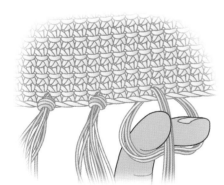

3 Pull through to make a big loop and, using your fingers, pull the tails of the bunch of strands through the loop.

4 Pull on the tails to tighten the loop firmly to secure the tassel.

Making a large tassel

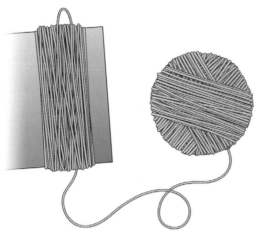

1 Cut a piece of cardboard or find something to wrap the yarn around which is the required length. I used my crochet hook case, which measures 17.5cm (7in).

Cut two strands of yarn before you start, one approx 90cm (36in) and another approx 45cm (18in) long. Wrap the remaining yarn neatly around the cardboard approx 200 times.

2 Take the 90cm (36in) length of yarn, fold in half and thread through all the loops at the top.

3 Hold this piece as you pull the loops off the cardboard, and tie tightly in a double knot.

4 Take the shorter length of yarn cut earlier and tie it around the tassel, approx 7.5cm (3in) from the top. Wrap around tightly several times and tie a tight knot.

Trim the ends.

5 Cut the loops at the bottom.

Making pompoms

BOOK METHOD

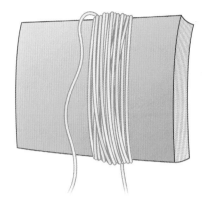

1 Leaving a long tail, wrap the yarn around a paperback book (or something a similar size) about 120 times, leaving a second long tail.

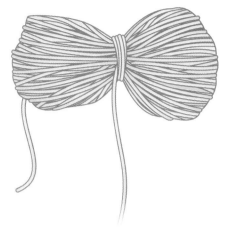

2 Ease the wrapped yarn off the book gently and wrap the second tail tightly around the centre six or seven times.

3 Take a yarn sewing needle and thread in the second tail. Push the needle through the centre wrap backwards and forwards three or four times.

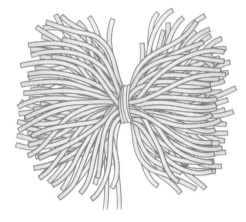

4 Cut the loops on each side of the wrap. Holding the two tails in one hand, hold the bobble and fluff it out.

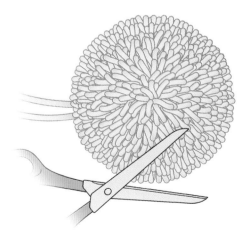

5 Hold the bobble in one hand and use sharp scissors to trim it into a round and even shape.

FORK METHOD

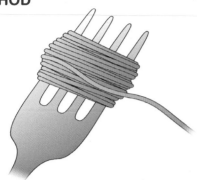

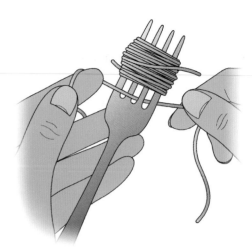

1 Keeping the yarn attached to the ball, wrap it around a fork about twenty times. Keep the wraps tight, and centre them in the middle of the fork, leaving space at the top and bottom.

2 Cut the yarn and hold the wraps in place on the fork. Cut a 7.5cm (3in) length of yarn and thread it through the middle of the fork at the bottom from front to back.

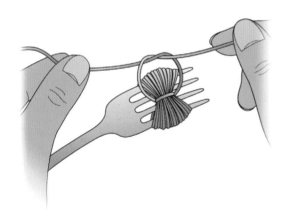

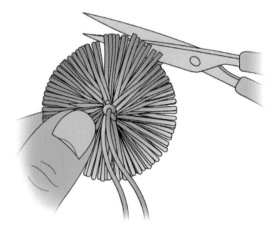

3 Wrap one end around and back over the top until the ends meet, then tie them tightly together at the front. Wrap the tie around the centre a few more times and tie another knot at the back.

4 Pull the wrap off the fork and pull the knot tighter. The wrap will begin to curl and turn flat and round. Tie another knot on top of the other one to secure. Use sharp embroidery scissors to cut the loops on either side of the tie.

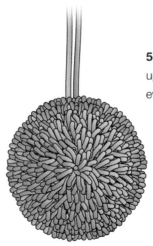

5 Trim the pompom and fluff it up until it's thick and a round, even shape.

CARDBOARD TUBE METHOD

1 Take two cardboard tubes, such as the inners of a toilet paper roll, and hold them together. Take the end of a ball of yarn and wrap it over the top of the top tube and between the tubes, then start wrapping around both tubes.

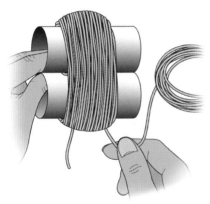

2 Carry on wrapping around both tubes, up to around 200 times for a nice fluffy pompom.

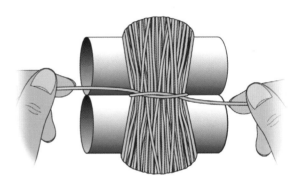

3 Cut the yarn, then cut a separate length of yarn 45cm (18in) long. Slide it between the two tubes and tie the ends.

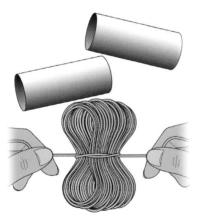

4 Slip the wrapped yarn gently off the tubes. Pull the tie tight, wrap the ends around the centre several times, pulling tightly each time, and tie with a double knot to secure.

5 Using sharp scissors, cut through the loops at each end of the wrap. Trim the ends of the pompom until it's thick, fluffy and round.

chapter one
cool colours

Materials

Debbie Bliss Baby Cashmerino, 55% wool/
33% acrylic/12% cashmere 4 ply yarn
50g (1¾oz) balls, approx 125m (137yd) per ball:
3 x balls of 202 Light Blue (blue)

3.5mm (US size E/4) crochet hook

Yarn sewing needle

Finished measurement

154cm (61½in) long

Tension

18 htr x 16 rows over a 10cm (4in) square
working half treble crochet using a 3.5mm
(US size E/4) hook and Debbie Bliss
Baby Cashmerino.

Abbreviations

approx approximately
ch chain
ch sp chain space
cont continu(e)(ing)
dc double crochet
htr half treble
rep repeat
RS right side
st(s) stitch(es)
ss slip stitch
tr treble

This is a wonderfully swishy scarf with a wavy edging. It would make a lovely transitional accessory to take you from the cooler to warmer months.

Scarf

Row 1: Make 258ch, 1htr in third ch from hook, 1htr in each ch to end. (256 sts)
Row 2: 2ch, 1htr in each st to end. (256 sts)
Do not fasten off.
Working in rounds from here on, cont working around on RS of work.

Edging round 1

Turn to work down side of work.
First short edge:
1ch, make 12dc evenly spaced along first edge.
First long edge:
Working on underside of ch, 1dc in each ch to end (making sure you go into every ch, particularly the first one).
Check at the end of this edge that you have 256 sts + 12 sts from First Short Edge.

Second short edge:
Make 12dc equally along second side edge.
Second long edge:
Make 1dc in each st to end.
Join with a ss in first dc. (536 sts)

Edging round 2

4ch (counts as 1tr, 1ch), [miss next st, 1tr in next st, 1ch]
5 times,
miss next st, [1tr, 1ch, 1tr, 1ch, 1tr] in next tr, (first
corner group),
*1ch, miss next st, 1tr in next st; rep from * to 3 sts before
next corner (126 tr from corner group)
miss next st, 1ch, [1tr, 1ch, 1tr, 1ch, 1tr] in next tr, (second
corner group),
[1ch, miss next st, 1tr in next st] 6 times, to third corner st.
miss next st, 1ch, [1tr, 1ch, 1tr, 1ch, 1tr] in next tr,
(third corner group),
*1ch, miss next st, 1tr in next st; rep from last * to last
corner st (2 sts before end), (count 126 trs from last corner
st) miss next st, 1ch, [1tr, 1ch, 1tr, 1ch, 1tr] in next tr,
(fourth corner group),
1ch, join with a ss in third of first 4-ch. (126 tr on each
length, 6 tr on each short ends plus 3tr in each 4 corner
groups) (276 tr)
NOTE: It's important to count stitches on this round.

Edging round 3

3ch (counts as 1 dc, 2 ch), miss first ch sp, 1htr in next tr,
2ch, miss next ch sp and miss next tr, 3tr in next
ch sp, 2ch, miss next tr, miss next ch sp, 1htr in next tr,
2ch, miss next ch sp, miss next tr, 1dc in next ch sp, 2ch,
miss next tr, miss next ch sp,
*1htr in next tr, 2ch, miss next ch sp, miss next tr,
1tr in next ch sp, 2ch, miss next tr, miss next ch sp,
1htr in next tr, 2ch, miss next ch sp, miss next tr,
1dc in next ch sp, 2ch, miss next tr, miss next ch sp **;
rep from * to centre ch sp at centre of short end, 3tr in
centre ch sp; rep from * to ** to end, omitting last dc,
join with a ss in first of first 3-ch.

Edging round 4

3ch (counts as 1dc, 2ch), 1dc in next htr, 2ch, 1tr in next
tr, [1tr, 1ch, 1tr, 1ch, 1tr] in next tr, 1tr in next tr, *2ch, 1dc
in next htr, 2ch, 1dc in next dc, 2ch, 1dc in next htr, 2ch,
[1tr, 1ch, 1tr, 1ch, 1tr] in next tr; rep from * along length
to 3-tr group at centre of short end, 2ch, 1tr in next tr,
[1tr, 1ch, 1tr, 1ch, 1tr] in next tr, 1tr in next tr; rep from *
to end, ending 1dc in last htr, 2ch, join with a ss in first of
first 3-ch.

Edging round 5

5ch (counts as 1tr, 2ch), miss next dc, [1tr in each of next 2tr, 3tr in next ch sp, 1ch, miss next tr, 3tr in next ch sp, 1tr in each of next 2tr], 2ch, miss next dc, 3tr in next dc, 2ch, miss next dc;

*[1tr in next tr, 3tr in next ch sp, 1ch, 3tr in next ch sp, 1tr in next tr],

**1ch, miss next dc, 1tr in next dc, 1ch, miss next dc; rep from * along first length ending last rep before short end at **,

2ch, miss next dc, 3tr in next dc, 2ch, miss next dc; [1tr in each of next 2tr, 3tr in next ch sp, 1ch, 3tr in next ch sp, 1tr in each of next 2tr], 2ch, miss next dc, 1tr in next dc, 2ch;

*miss next dc, [1tr in next tr, 3tr in next ch sp, 1ch, 3tr in next ch sp, 1tr in next tr], 1ch, miss next dc, 1tr in next dc, 1ch;

rep from last * along second length, ending 2ch, 2tr in same place as first 5ch, join with a ss in third of first 5-ch.

Edging round 6

Ss in first ch sp, 1ch, 1dc in next tr, miss next 2tr, [7tr in next tr, miss next tr, 1dc in next ch sp, miss next tr, 7tr in next tr], miss next 2tr, 1dc in next tr, miss next tr (of 3-tr group), 3tr in centre tr (of 3-tr group), miss next tr (of 3-tr group),

*1dc in next tr, miss 1tr, [7tr in next tr, miss next tr, 1dc in next ch sp, miss next tr, 7tr in next tr] miss next tr, 1dc in next tr, miss next tr; rep from * along length to 3-tr group before short end, miss first tr (of 3-tr group), 3tr in centre tr (of 3-tr group), miss next tr (of 3-tr group), 1dc in next tr, miss each of next 2tr, [7tr in next tr, 1dc in next ch sp, miss next tr, 7tr in next tr], miss next 2tr, 1dc in next tr, miss next tr (of next 3-tr group), 3tr in centre st (of 3-tr group) miss next tr (of 3-tr group); rep from * again to 3tr-group before second short end, miss next tr (of next 3-tr group), 3tr in centre st (of 3-tr group), miss next tr (of 3-tr group), join with a ss in first dc.
Fasten off.

Finishing

Sew in ends.

shimmer
scarf

This exquisite scarf is made up of two different types of squares sewn together. The yarn I've used is a beautiful mix of silk and merino, which is a pleasure to crochet. The squares can look a little crumpled until they are blocked and pressed.

Materials

Fyberspates Scrumptious 4 ply Sport, 55% merino/45% silk 4 ply yarn

100g (3½oz) skeins, approx 365m (399yd) per skein: 2 x skeins of 318 Glisten (grey)

3mm (US size C/2–D/3) crochet hook

Yarn sewing needle

Finished measurement

20cm (8in) wide x 163cm (64in) long

Tension

Each square measures approx 10cm (4in) square, using a 3mm (US size C/2–D/3) hook and Fyberspates Scrumptious 4 ply Sport.

Abbreviations

approx approximately
ch chain
ch sp chain space
CL cluster
dc double crochet
dtr double treble
htr half treble
rep repeat
RS right side
st(s) stitch(es)
ss slip stitch
tr treble
yrh yarn round hook

Special abbreviations

2trCL (2 treble cluster): *yrh, insert hook in next st, yrh, pull yarn through, yrh, pull through 2 loops, rep from * once more, yrh, pull yarn through all 3 loops on hook.
3trCL (3 treble cluster): *yrh, insert hook in next st, yrh, pull yarn through, yrh, pull through 2 loops, rep from * twice more, yrh, pull yarn through all 4 loops on hook.
5trCL (5 treble cluster): *yrh, insert hook in next st, yrh, pull yarn through, yrh, pull through 2 loops, rep from * 4 times more, yrh, pull yarn through all 6 loops on hook.
6trCL (6 treble cluster): *yrh, insert hook in next st, yrh, pull yarn through, yrh, pull through 2 loops, rep from * 5 times more, yrh, pull yarn through all 7 loops on hook.

Daisy square

(make 16)

Make 4ch, join with a ss in first ch to form a ring.

Round 1: 1ch, 8dc in ring, join with a ss in first dc. (8 sts)

Round 2: 3ch, 2trCL in same st (counts as first CL), [3ch, 3trCL in next st] 7 times, 3ch, ss in top of first CL. (8 CL)

Round 3: 3ch, 1tr in same place as ss (counts as first CL), *miss 3ch, [2trCL, 5ch, 2trCL] all in top of next CL; rep from * 6 more times, 2trCL in first CL from second round, 5ch, ss in top of first 3-ch.

Round 4: Ss in top of next CL, 7ch (counts as 1tr and 4ch), [1dc in next 5-ch sp, 4ch, miss 1 CL, 1tr in next CL, 4ch] 7 times, 1dc in next 5-ch sp, 4ch, ss in third of first 7-ch.

Round 5: 1ch, 1dc in same place, *4ch, miss 4-ch sp, [1dtr, 4ch, 1dtr] into next dc, 4ch, miss 4-ch sp, 1dc in next tr, 4ch, miss 4-ch sp, 1htr in next dc, 4ch, miss 4ch, 1dc in next tr; rep from * 3 more times, omitting dc at end of last rep, ss in first dc. (20 sps)

Round 6: Ss in next 4-ch sp, 4dc in next 4-ch sp, *1dc in top of next dtr, 4ch in next 4-ch sp, 1dc in top of next dtr, 4dc in each of next four 4-ch sps; rep from * twice more, 1dc in top of next dtr, 4ch in next 4-ch sp, 1dc in top of next dtr, 4dc in each of next three 4-ch sps, join with a ss in top of first dc. (88 sts)

Fasten off.

4-petal flower square

(make 16)

Make 10ch, join with a ss to form a ring.

Round 1: 3ch (counts as 1tr), 4tr in ring, [7ch, 5tr in ring] 3 times, 7ch, join with a ss in top of first 3-ch.

Round 2: 3ch, 1tr in first tr, 2tr in next tr, 1tr in each of next 2tr, *[2ch, 3tr, 5ch, 3tr, 2ch] in next 7-ch sp, 1tr in each of next 2tr, 2tr in next tr, 1tr in each of next 2tr: rep from * twice more, [2ch, 3tr, 5ch, 3tr, 2ch] in next 7-ch sp, join with a ss in top of first 3-ch.

Round 3: 2ch, 5trCL over next 5tr, *5ch, miss next 2-ch sp and next tr, 1tr in next tr (in centre of 3-tr group), miss next tr, [3ch, 2tr, 2ch, 2tr, 3ch] in next 5-ch sp, miss next tr, 1tr in next tr, miss 2-ch sp, 5ch, 6trCL over next 6 tr; rep from * twice more, 5ch, miss next 2-ch sp and next tr, 1tr in next tr (in centre of 3-tr group), miss next tr, [3ch, 2tr, 2ch, 2tr, 3ch] in next 5-ch sp, miss next tr, 1tr in next tr, miss 2-ch sp, 5ch, join with a ss in top of first 2-ch.

Round 4: 1ch, 1dc in first CL, *3dc in next 5-ch sp, 1dc in next tr, 3dc in next 3-ch sp, 1dc in each of next 2-tr, 3dc in next 2-ch sp (corner), 1dc in each of next 2-tr, 3dc in next 3-ch sp, 1dc in next tr, 3dc in next 5-ch sp, 1dc in top of next CL; rep from * to end, ending last rep with a ss in top of first 1dc (top of CL). (88 sts)

Fasten off.

Finishing

Pin and block squares lightly on WS.

Lay out squares with one Daisy square and one 4-petal square side by side, in a row of two, and alternating Daisy and 4-petal squares in each row.

With RS together, sew pairs of squares along length of scarf, then sew pairs together.

Edging

With RS facing, join yarn in dc at top of second dtr of any corner of Daisy Square.

1ch, 1dc in same st, 1ch, * miss next 2 sts, 1tr in next st, 4ch, ss in third ch from hook, 1ch, 1tr in same st, 1ch, miss next 2 sts, 1dc in next st, 1ch; rep from * around scarf edge, ending 1tr in last st, 4ch, ss in third ch from hook, 1ch, 1tr in same st, 1ch, ss in top of first dc.

Fasten off.

Tip

When you are using this yarn, always wind skeins into a ball before crocheting.

lagoon
chunky scarf

A wonderfully soft and chunky yarn makes this a really gorgeous project for the depths of winter. This is the perfect scarf if you're a beginner and want to practise your double crochet.

Materials

Debbie Bliss Lara, chunky/super chunky yarn
58% merino wool/42% superfine alpaca
100g (3½oz) balls, approx 60m (65yd) per ball:
3 x balls of 10 Marya (blue) (A)
1 x ball of 01 Pasha (off white) (B)

10mm (US size N/15) crochet hook

Yarn sewing needle

Finished measurement

15cm (6in) wide x 210cm (84in) long
(including pompoms)

Tension

Approx 7 sts x 7 rows over a 10cm (4in) square
working double crochet using a 10mm (US size
N/15) hook and Debbie Bliss Lara.

Abbreviations

approx approximately
ch chain
dc double crochet
rep repeat
st(s) stitch(es)

Method

Row 1: Using A, make 12ch, 1dc in second ch from hook, 1dc in each ch to end. (11 sts)

Row 2: 1ch, 1dc in each st to end. (11 sts)

Rep Row 2 until work measures approx 200cm (80in).

Fasten off.

Finishing

Sew in ends using a yarn sewing needle with a large eye. If you don't have one of these, you can use a smaller crochet hook and pull the ends through a few stitches to finish off.

Using B, make 6 pompoms, 5cm (2in) wide (see Book Method, page 29) and attach 3 at each end, one in each corner and one in the middle.

scarf

Materials
Louisa Harding Amitola, 80% wool/20% silk
DK yarn
50g (1¾oz) balls, approx 250m (273yd) per ball:
5 x balls of 123 Morgan (cream/green/blue)

3.5mm (US size E/4) crochet hook

Yarn sewing needle

Finished measurement
Approx 30cm (12in) wide x 178cm (70in) long

Tension
Approx 3½ fans x 8 fan rows over a 10cm (4in)
square, working fantail stitch using a 3.5mm
(US size E/4) hook and Louisa Harding Amitola.

Abbreviations
approx approximately
ch chain
ch sp chain space
dc double crochet
htr half treble
rep repeat
RS right side
st(s) stitch(es)
tch turning chain
tr treble

Special abbreviations
Fan: [3tr, 1ch, 3tr]
V-st: [1htr, 1ch, 1htr]

Note
Tension is worked loosely, adjust your hook and
tension accordingly.

The colours and the softness of this yarn just remind me of being by the beach near my home. You will love working with this yarn – the colours slowly change as they slip through your fingers; it's a joy to work with.

Scarf

Row 1 (RS): Make 102ch (Foundation chain), 1dc in second ch from hook, 1dc in next ch, *miss 3ch, work a Fan in next ch, miss 3ch, 1dc in next ch**, 1ch, miss 1ch, 1dc in next ch; rep from * ending last rep at **, 1dc in last ch.

Row 2: 2ch (counts as 1htr), 1htr in first st, *3ch, 1dc in 1-ch sp at centre of next Fan, 3ch**, work a V-st in next ch sp (between 1dc, 1ch, 1dc from previous row); rep from * ending last rep at **, 2htr in last dc.

Row 3: 3ch (counts as 1tr), 3tr in first st, *1dc in next 3-ch sp, 1ch, 1dc in next 3-ch sp **, work a Fan in 1-ch sp at centre of next V-st; rep from * ending last rep at **, 4tr in top of tch.

Row 4: 1ch, 1dc in first st, *3ch, V-st in next ch sp, 3ch, 1dc in 1-ch sp at centre of next Fan; rep from * ending last rep in top of tch.

Row 5: 1ch, 1dc in first st, *1dc in next ch sp, Fan in ch sp at centre of next V-st, 1dc in next ch sp **, 1ch; rep from * ending last rep at **, 1dc in last dc.

Rep Rows 2, 3, 4 and 5 until work measures approx 178cm (70in) ending on a Row 5.
Fasten off.

Edging

Edge 1:

(work on underside of Foundation chain of Row 1)

Row 1: With RS facing, join yarn in first dc on underside of Foundation chain. 1ch, 1dc in same st, miss next ch sp, 1ch, 7tr in space made at the base of the first Fan, miss next ch sp, *1ch, 1dc in sp between [1dc, 1ch, 1dc] of Row 1, miss next ch sp, 1ch, 7tr in space made at the base of the next Fan, miss next ch sp; rep from * ending 1ch, 1dc in base of last dc.

Row 2: 3ch, 1dc in first tr, *[4ch, miss next tr, 1dc in next tr] 3 times**, 4ch, miss next [1ch, 1dc, 1ch], 1dc in next tr; rep from * ending last rep at **, 3ch, 1dc in last dc.

Fasten off.

Edge 2:

Row 1: With RS facing, join yarn in first dc, 1ch, 1dc in same st, *1ch, 7tr in 1-ch sp in centre of Fan, 1ch, 1dc in next 1-ch sp between [1dc, 1ch, 1dc]; rep from * ending 1ch, 1dc in last dc.

Row 2: Rep Row 2 from Edge 1.

Fasten off.

Finishing

Sew in ends.

Brighton sky
bobble scarf

This scarf has posts and bobbles going up the middle, and is made using a beautiful soft yarn in variegated colours.

Materials

Louisa Harding Amitola Grande, 80% wool/20% silk chunky yarn

100g (3½oz) balls, approx 250m (273yd) per ball:

1 x ball of 527 Amelia (blue/pink/grey)

5mm (US size H/8) crochet hook

Yarn sewing needle

Finished measurement

Approx 18cm (7in) wide x 188cm (74in) long

Tension

Approx 16 sts x 5 rows over a 10cm (4in) square, working trebles using a 5mm (US size H/8) hook and Louisa Harding Amitola Grande.

Abbreviations

approx approximately
ch chain
ch sp chain space
dc double crochet
dtr double treble
foll following
rep repeat(ed)
st(s) stitch(es)
tr treble
yrh yarn round hook

Special abbreviations

5trCL (5 treble cluster): *yrh, insert hook in next st, yrh, pull yarn through, yrh, pull through 2 loops, rep from * 4 times more, yrh, pull yarn through all 6 loops on hook.

fpdtr (front post double treble/raised double treble round front): working on stitch from previous round, yrh twice and insert the hook from the front and around the post (the stem) of the next treble from right to left.
Yrh and pull the yarn through the work (4 loops on hook), yrh and pull the yarn through the first 2 loops on the hook (3 loops on hook).
Yrh and pull the yarn through the 2 loops on the hook (2 loops on hook).
Yrh, pull yarn through the remaining 2 loops on the hook.
(One raised double treble round front completed.)

Scarf

Row 1: Make 31 ch, 1tr in fourth ch from hook (counts as 1tr), 1tr in each of next 10 ch, [1ch, miss next ch, 1tr in next ch] 3 times, 1tr in each of last 11 ch. (29 sts)

Row 2: 1ch, 1dc in each of next 12 sts, 5trCL in next ch sp (bobble), 1dc in next tr, 1dc in next ch sp, 1dc in next tr, 5trCL in next ch sp, 1dc in each of last 12 sts.

Row 3: 3ch (counts as 1tr), miss first dc, 1tr in each of next 7 dc, 1fpdtr round next tr of row below the next dc (on foll rep Row 3, make this fpdtr around corresponding fpdtr below the next dc), 1tr in next dc from previous row, 1fpdtr round next tr of row below the next dc (on foll rep Row 3, make this fpdtr around corresponding fpdtr below the next dc), 1ch, miss next dc, 1tr in closing chain of first bobble, 1ch, miss next dc, 1tr in next dc (centre dc between bobbles), 1ch, miss next dc, 1tr in closing chain of next bobble, 1ch, miss next tr from 2 rows below, 1fpdtr round next tr of row below the next dc (on foll rep Row 3, make this fpdtr around the

corresponding fpdtr below the next dc), 1tr in next dc from previous row, 1fpdtr round next tr of row below the next dc (on foll rep Row 3, make this fpdtr around corresponding fpdtr below the next dc), 1tr in each of last 8 dc. (8tr on each end, before and after the first and last fpdtr posts)

Row 4: 1ch, 1dc in each of the next 11 sts, 1dc in next ch sp, 1dc in next tr, 1dc in next ch sp, 5trCL in next tr, 1dc in next ch sp, 1dc in next tr, 1dc in next ch sp, 1dc in each of next 10 sts, 1dc in top of first 3-ch from previous row.

Row 5: 3ch (counts as 1tr), miss first dc, 1tr in each of next 7 dc, 1fpdtr round next corresponding fpdtr of row below the next dc, 1tr in next dc on previous row, 1fpdtr round next corresponding fpdtr of row below the next dc, 1tr in next dc on previous row, 1ch, miss next dc, 1tr in next dc (before bobble), 1ch, miss bobble, 1tr in next dc (on other side of bobble), 1ch, miss next dc, 1tr in next dc, 1fpdtr round next corresponding fpdtr of row below the next dc, 1tr in next dc from previous row, 1fpdtr round next corresponding fpdtr of row below the next dc, 1tr in each of next 8 dc.

Rep Rows 2–5 until work measures approx 188cm (74in), ending on a Row 3 or 5.

Fasten off.

Finishing

Sew in ends.

Tips

Make sure you end each 5trCL with 1ch to close the cluster.

Don't forget to make a double treble around the posts and not a treble.

glisten
cowl

Gorgeous, fluffy and flouncy – this mohair isn't the mohair of old, it's really soft and silky. Wrap it twice around your neck and it will look fantastic and keep you lovely and warm too.

Materials

Debbie Bliss Angel, 76% super kid mohair/24% silk lace weight
25g (⅞oz) balls, approx 200m (219yd) per ball:
2 x balls of 09 Aqua (blue) (MC)
1 x ball of 41 Citrus (yellow) (A)

4mm (US size G/6) crochet hook

Yarn sewing needle

Finished measurement

30cm (12in) wide x 120cm (48in), without edging

Tension

24 sts (2 patterns) x 12 rows over a 10cm (4in) square, using a 4mm (US size G/6) hook and Debbie Bliss Angel.

Abbreviations

approx approximately
ch chain
ch sp chain space
dc double crochet
rep repeat
RS right side
st(s) stitch(es)
ss slip stitch
tch turning chain
tr treble

Cowl

Row 1 (RS): Using MC, make 279ch, 2tr in third ch from hook, *miss 2ch, 1dc in next ch, 5ch, miss 5ch, 1dc in next ch, miss 2ch, 5tr in next ch; rep from * ending last rep with only 3tr in last ch.

Row 2: 1ch, 1dc in first st, *5ch, 1dc in next 5-ch sp, 5ch, 1dc in third tr of next 5-tr group; rep from * ending last rep with 1dc in top of tch.

Row 3: *5ch, 1dc in next 5-ch sp, 5tr in next dc, 1dc in next ch sp; rep from * ending 2ch, 1tr in last dc, miss tch.

Row 4: 1ch, 1dc in first st, *5ch, 1dc in third tr of next 5-tr group, 5ch, 1dc in next 5-ch sp; rep from * ending last dc in 3rd ch of last 5-ch sp.

Row 5: 3ch (counts as 1tr), 2tr in first st, *1dc in next 5-ch sp, 5ch, 1dc in next 5-ch sp, 5tr in next dc; rep from * ending last rep with only 3tr in last dc, miss tch.

Rep Rows 2, 3, 4 and 5 eight times and then Row 2 once.

Fasten off.

With RS together, join side seam using MC. Turn right side out.

Bottom edging

With RS facing, join MC on Row 1 at the seam and make 5dc in each 5-ch sp, 1dc in base ch of each dc, 2dc in each 2-ch sp, 1dc in base ch of 5tr group to end. (276 sts)

Join with a ss in first dc.

Fasten off.

Top edging

With RS facing, join MC at seam of final row and make 5dc in each 5-ch sp, 1dc in in each dc to end. (276 sts)

Join with a ss in first dc.

Fasten off.

Frill edge (both edges)

With RS facing, join A, 1dc in same st, *20ch, ss in next st, 10ch, ss in next st; rep from * around, join with a ss in first dc. Fasten off.

Finishing

Sew in ends.

Tip

This is an easy stitch to work, but because it's in mohair it's difficult to undo if you make a mistake. Practise the stitch first on some non-hairy wool.

This scarf is made using a colourful mix of silk and soft wool, which is a beautiful yarn to work with and feels very smooth on the skin. The stitch is a wave and chevron stitch using trebles, with flashes of bright colour in between the blocks of colour in double crochet.

Materials

Fyberspates Scrumptious 4 ply Sport, 55% merino/45% silk 4 ply yarn 100g (3½oz) skeins, apprcx 365m (399yd) per skein:

1 x skein each of:
318 Glisten (silver) (A)
308 Teal Blue (dark blue) (B)
302 Gold (gold) (C)
310 Natural (white) (D)
304 Water (pale blue) (E)
320 Burnt Orange (bronze) (F)
303 Oyster (beige) (G)

3mm (US size C/2–D/3) and 4mm (US size G/6) crochet hooks

Yarn sewing needle

Finished measurement

25cm (10in) wide x 202cm (79½in) long

Tension

24 sts x 9 rows over 10cm (4in) square, working Wave & Chevron stitch using 3mm (US size C/2–D/3) hook and Fyberspates Scrumptious 4 ply Sport.

Abbreviations

approx approximately
ch chain
cont continu(e)(ing)
dc double crochet
rep repeat
RS right side
st(s) stitch(es)
tr treble
yrh yarn round hook

Special abbreviations

tr3tog (treble crochet 3 stitches together):
*yrh, insert hook in next st, yrh, pull yarn through, yrh, pull yarn through 2 loops on hook (2 loops on hook). Rep from * in each of next 2 sts (4 loops on hook), yrh, pull yarn through all 4 loops on hook.

dc3tog (double crochet 3 stitches together):
insert hook in next st, yrh, pull yarn through (2 loops on hook), insert hook in next st, yrh, pull yarn through (3 loops on hook), insert hook in next st, yrh, pull yarn through (4 loops on hook), yrh, pull yarn through all 4 loops on hook.

TrRow: Wave & Chevron Treble Stitch row.
DcRow: Wave & Chevron Double Crochet Stitch row.

Scarf

TrRow 1: Using A and 4mm (US size G/6) hook, make 63ch, change to 3mm (US size C/2–D/3) hook, 1tr in third ch from hook (first 2 ch count as 1tr), 1tr in each of next 3ch, tr3tog over next 3 ch, 1tr in each of next 3 ch, *3tr in next ch, 1tr in each of next 3 ch, tr3tog over next 3 ch, 1tr in each of next 3 ch; rep from * to last ch, 2tr in last ch.

TrRow 2: 3ch (count as 1tr), 1tr in each of first 4 sts, tr3tog over next 3 sts, 1tr in each of next 3 sts, *3tr in next st, 1tr in each of next 3 sts, tr3tog over next 3 sts, 1tr in each of next 3 sts; rep from * to end, 2tr in top of 3-ch at end of row.

Rep TrRow 2 until 28 rows have been worked or work measures approx 30cm (12in).

Cut yarn, do not fasten off.

DcRow1: Using 4mm (US size G/6) hook, join B, 1ch (counts as first dc), 1dc in each of first 4 sts, dc3tog over next 3 sts, 1dc in each of next 3 sts, *3dc in next st, 1dc in each of next 3 sts, dc3tog over next 3 sts, 1dc in each of next 3 sts; rep from * to end, 2dc in top of 3-ch at end of row.

DcRow2: Join C, 1ch (counts as first dc), 1dc in each of first 4 sts, dc3tog over next 3 sts, 1dc in each of next 3 sts, *3dc in next st, 1dc in each of next 3 sts, dc3tog over next 3 sts, 1dc in each of next 3 sts; rep from * to end, 2dc in top of 1-ch at end of row.

DcRow3: Join D, rep DcRow2 once more.

Cut yarn, do not fasten off.

*Using 3mm (US size C/2–D/3) hook, join E.

Rep TrRow2 until 28 rows have been worked or work measures approx 30cm (12in), and ending first row with 2tr in top of 1-ch, and following rows with 2tr in top of 3-ch at end of row.**

Using 4mm (US size G/6) hook, rep DcRows 1–3 using B, C and D in any order.*

Rep from * to * 4 times more, ending last rep at **, following colour sequence F, G, E, A for TrRows.

Fasten off.

Finishing

Sew in ends and press lightly using a damp cloth.

Tips

When you are using this yarn, always wind skeins into a ball before crocheting.

Make sure that you go into the first stitch at the beginning and end of the rows, and make the two trebles into the top of the third chain from the previous row.

At the end of each 2-row colour sequence, cut the yarn – but do not fasten off – and join in the new colour.

samphire
scarf

This is a lovely scarf for wearing in spring or summer. It's made using a fine yarn with a silk blend and has shaping that ties around the front – it can also be draped around the shoulders for breezy summer evenings outside. This beaded pattern is for the more experienced crocheter – it needs to be followed very carefully and each row is different. But it's well worth the effort, because the end result is a beautiful scarf.

Materials

Fyberspates Scrumptious 4 ply Sport, 55% merino/45% silk 4 ply yarn 100g (3½oz) skeins, approx 365m (399yd) per skein:

2 x skeins of 311 Flying Saucer (pale green)

370 x white seed beads, size 6

3mm (US size C/2–D/3) crochet hook

Yarn sewing needle

Finished measurement

110cm (44in) wide x 36.5cm (14½in) long (at longest point)

Tension

3 shell group (Row 5) x 12 rows (2 patt repeats) measures 10cm (4in), using 3mm (US size C/2–D/3) hook and Fyberspates Scrumptious 4 ply Sport.

Abbreviations

approx approximately
ch chain
ch sp chain space
dc double crochet
dc2tog double crochet 2 stitches together
htr half treble
htr2tog half treble 2 stitches together
rep repeat
RS right side
ss slip stitch
st(s) stitch(es)
tr treble
tr2tog treble 2 stitches together
WS wrong side

Special abbreviations

V-st: [1tr, 1ch, 1tr]
PB: place bead

Scarf

Row 1 (Foundation chain): Make 308ch, 1tr in sixth ch from hook, 1ch, 1tr in same ch, *miss next 3 ch, 1ch, [1tr, 1ch, 1tr] (V-st) in next ch; rep from * to last 2 ch, miss next ch, 1tr in last ch.

Row 2: *5ch, 1dc in next ch sp (centre of V-st); rep from * to end, 2ch, 1tr in top of first 6-ch.

Row 3: 3ch, 1tr in next 5-ch sp, 2ch, *1dc in next 5-ch sp, 2ch, 3tr in next ch sp, 2ch; rep from * to last two 5-ch sps, 1tr in next 5-ch sp, 1tr in last 5-ch sp.

Row 4: 3ch, [1tr, 1ch] in first tr of first 3-tr group, [1tr, 1ch] twice in next tr (centre of 3-tr group), [1tr, 1ch] in next tr (of last 3-tr group), *[1tr, 1ch] in first tr (of next 3-tr group), [1tr, 1ch] twice in next tr (centre of 3-tr group), [1tr, 1ch] in next tr (of last 3-tr group); rep from * to last tr, 1tr in last tr.

Row 5: 1ch, miss first tr and next tr of first 4-tr group, 1dc in first ch sp (of 4-tr group), [1htr, 2tr] in next ch sp, 2tr in next ch sp, 1dc in next ch sp, *2tr in next ch sp, 3tr in next ch sp, 2tr in next ch sp, 1dc in next ch sp; rep from * to last 4-tr group, 2tr in next ch sp, [2tr, 1htr] in next ch sp, 1dc in last ch sp.

Row 6: Ss in first dc, ss in next htr, 1ch, 1dc in each of next 2 tr, *2ch, miss next 2-tr, 1tr in next dc (between tr groups), 2ch**, miss next 2-tr, 1dc in each of next 3-tr; rep from * ending at ** (before last tr group), miss next 2-tr, 1dc in each of next 2-tr.

Row 7: 3ch, 1tr in first ch sp, [1ch, 1tr] twice in next ch sp, 1ch, *[1tr, 1ch] twice in next ch sp; rep from * to last ch sp, 1tr in last ch sp, 1tr in first 1-ch from previous row.

Row 8: 5ch, miss first ch sp, 1dc in next ch sp (between V-st), *5ch, miss next ch sp, 1dc in next ch sp (between V-sts); rep from * to end, 2ch, miss last ch sp, 1tr in last tr.

Row 9: 1ch, dc2tog over first tr and first 5-ch sp, *2ch, 3tr in next 5-ch sp, 2ch**, 1dc in next 5-ch sp; rep from * ending at **, dc2tog over last two 5-ch sps.

Row 10: 2ch, 1dc in first tr, 1ch, [1htr, 1ch, 1tr] in next tr, 1ch, 1tr in next tr, *miss next [ch sp, dc, ch sp], [1ch, 1tr] in next tr (of 3-tr group), [1ch, 1tr] twice in next tr (centre of 3-tr group), [1ch, 1tr] in next tr (last tr of 3-tr group); rep from * to last 3-tr group, 1ch, 1tr in first tr, 1ch, [1tr, 1ch, 1htr] in next tr, 1ch, 1dc in next tr, 1tr in dc2tog from previous row.

Row 11: Ss in first tr, ss in first dc, ss in first ch sp, ss in next htr, ss in next ch sp, ss in next tr, 2ch, 1htr in next ch sp, 1dc in next ch sp, *2tr in next ch sp, 3tr in next ch sp, 2tr in next ch sp, 1dc in next ch sp; rep from *, htr2tog over next ch sp and last tr.

Row 12: 2ch, 1tr in first dc, 1ch, miss next 2 tr, *1dc in each of next 3 tr, 2ch**, miss next 2 tr, 1tr in next dc, 2ch, miss next 2 tr; rep from * ending last rep at **, tr2tog over next dc and next htr.

Row 13: 3ch, miss first ch sp, miss next 3 dc, *[1tr, 1ch] twice in next 2-ch sp; rep from * to end, omitting 1ch of last rep, miss last 1-ch sp, 1tr in last tr.

Row 14: 3ch, 1tr in first ch sp (centre of V-st), 2ch, miss next ch sp, 1dc in next ch sp (centre of V-st), *5ch, miss next ch sp, 1dc in next ch sp (centre of V-st); rep from * to last 2 V-sts, 1dc in centre of next V-st, 2ch, miss next ch sp, tr2tog over next ch sp (centre of V-st) and top of first 3-ch from previous row.

Row 15: 5ch, 1dc in next 5-ch sp, *2ch, 3tr in next 5-ch sp, 2ch**, 1dc in next 5-ch sp; rep from * to last 5-ch sp ending at **, 1dc in last 2-ch sp, 2ch, 1tr in last tr.

Row 16: 3ch, miss first 2-ch sp, miss next dc, miss next 5-ch sp, 1tr in first tr (of 3-tr group), [1ch, 1tr] twice in next tr, (centre of 3-tr group) [1ch, 1tr] in next tr (last tr of 3-tr group), *miss next [ch sp, dc, ch sp], [1ch, 1tr] in next tr (of 3-tr group), [1ch, 1tr] twice in next tr (centre of 3-tr group), [1ch, 1tr] in next tr (last tr of 3-tr group); rep from * to last 3-tr group, 1ch, 1tr in first tr, [1ch, 1tr] twice in next tr, 1ch, tr2tog over last tr and third of first 5-ch.

Row 17: 1ch, dc2tog over first tr2tog and next tr, [1htr, 2tr] in next ch sp (between centre V-sts), 2tr in next ch sp, 1dc in next ch sp, *2tr in next ch sp, 3tr in next ch sp, 2tr in next ch sp, 1dc in next ch sp; rep from * to last tr group, 2tr in next ch sp, [2tr, 1htr] in next ch sp, dc2tog over last ch sp and last tr.

Row 18: Ss in top of dc2tog from previous row, ss in next htr, 1ch, 1dc in each of next 2 tr, *2ch, miss next 2 tr, 1tr in next dc **, 2ch, miss next 2 tr**, 1dc in each of next 3 tr; rep from * ending at ** before last tr group, 1dc in each of last 2tr.

Row 19: 3ch, 1tr in first ch sp, [1tr, 1ch, 1tr] (V-st) in next ch sp, *miss next 3dc, 1ch, [1tr, 1ch, 1tr] (V-st) in next ch sp, miss next tr, 1ch, [1tr, 1ch, 1tr] (V-st) in next ch sp; rep from * to last ch sp, tr2tog over last ch sp and last dc from previous row.

Row 20: 5ch, 1dc in first ch sp (between first V-st), *5ch, miss next ch sp, 1dc in next ch sp (between next V-st); rep from * to end, 1tr in last tr.

Row 21: 3ch, 1tr in first 5-ch sp, 3tr in next ch sp, *2ch, 1dc in next ch sp, 2ch, 3tr in next ch sp; rep from * to last two 5-ch sps, tr2tog over last two 5-ch sps.

Row 22: 3ch, miss first tr2tog from previous row, tr2tog over first 2-tr (of first 3-tr group), 1tr in same tr, 1ch, 1tr in next tr (last tr of 3-tr group), 1ch, *miss next [ch sp, dc, ch sp], [1tr, 1ch] in next tr (first of 3-tr group), [1tr, 1ch] twice in next tr (centre of 3-tr group), [1tr, 1ch] in next tr (last of 3-tr group); rep from * to last 3-tr group, 1tr, 1ch in next tr (first of 3-tr group), 1tr in next tr (centre of 3-tr group), tr3tog over same tr and last 2-tr.

Row 23: 3ch, 1htr in first ch sp, *1dc in next ch sp, 2tr in next ch sp, 3tr in next ch sp, 2tr in next ch sp; rep from * to last ch sp, 1htr in last ch sp, 1tr in top of first 3-ch.

Row 24: 2ch, 1tr in first dc, *2ch, miss next 2 tr, 1dc in each of next 3 tr, 2ch**, miss next 2 tr, 1tr in next dc; rep from * ending last rep at **, miss next 2 tr, tr2tog over last dc and top of first 3-ch.

Row 25: 3ch, 1tr in first ch sp, 1ch, *miss next 3-dc, [1tr, 1ch] twice in next ch sp, miss next tr [1tr, 1ch] twice in next ch sp; rep from * to last 2 ch sps, tr2tog over last ch sp and last tr.

Row 26: *5ch, miss next ch sp, 1dc in next ch sp (centre of V-st); rep from * to last ch sp, miss last ch sp and last tr, 2ch, 1tr in top of last tr.

Row 27: 3ch, tr2tog in first 5-ch sp, *2ch, 1dc in next 5-ch sp, 2ch, 3tr in next 5-ch sp; rep from * to last 3 5-ch sps, 2ch, 1dc in next 5-ch ch sp, 2ch, tr3tog over last 2 5-ch sps.

Row 28: 3ch, *miss next [ch sp, dc, ch sp], [1tr, 1ch] in next tr (first of 3-tr group), [1tr, 1ch] twice in next tr (centre of 3-tr group), [1tr, 1ch] in next tr (last of 3-tr group); rep from * to last [ch sp, dc, ch sp], omit last 1ch from last rep, miss last [ch sp, dc, ch sp], 1tr in top of tr2tog from previous row.

Row 29: 1ch, 1dc in first tr, [1dc, 1htr] in first ch sp, 3tr in next ch sp, 2tr in next ch sp, 1dc in next ch sp, *2tr in next ch sp, 3tr in next ch sp, 2tr in next ch sp, 1dc in next ch sp; rep from * to last tr group, 2tr in next ch sp, 3tr in next ch sp, [1htr, 1dc] in last ch sp, 1dc in top of first 3-ch.

Row 30: Ss in each of first 2 dc, ss in next htr, 1ch, miss next tr, 1dc in each of next 2 tr, *2ch, miss next 2 tr, 1tr in next dc, 2ch, miss next 2 tr, 1dc in each of next 3 tr; rep from * to last dc, 2ch, 1tr in last dc, 2ch, miss next 2 tr, 1dc in each of next 2 tr.

Row 31: 3ch, 1tr in first ch sp, 1ch, [1tr, 1ch] twice in next ch sp, *miss next 3 dc, [1tr, 1ch] twice in next ch sp **, miss next tr, [1tr, 1ch] twice in next ch sp; rep from * to last ch sp, ending last rep at **, miss next tr, tr2tog over last ch sp and first ch from previous row.

Row 32: *5ch, miss first ch sp, 1dc in next ch sp (centre of V-st); rep from * to last ch sp, miss last ch sp, 1tr in top of last tr.

Row 33: 5ch, 1dc in first 5-ch sp, *2ch, 3tr in next 5-ch sp, 2ch, 1dc in next 5-ch sp; rep from * to last ch sp, 2ch, 1tr in last 5-ch sp.

Row 34: 3ch, miss next [ch sp, dc, ch sp], tr2tog over first 2 tr, 1ch, 1tr in same tr (centre of 3-tr group), 1ch, 1tr in next tr (last of 3-tr group), 1ch, *miss next [ch sp, dc, ch sp], [1tr, 1ch] in next tr (first of 3-tr group), [1tr, 1ch] twice in next tr (centre of 3-tr group), [1tr, 1ch] in next tr (last of 3-tr group); rep from * to last tr group, [1tr, 1ch] in next tr (first of 3-tr group), [1tr, 1ch] in next tr (centre of 3-tr group), tr3tog over same tr, last tr and third of first 5-ch from previous row.

Row 35: 3ch, tr2tog over first two 1-ch sps, 1tr in same sp, 1dc in next ch sp, *2tr in next ch sp, 3tr in next ch sp, 2tr in next ch sp, 1dc in next ch sp; rep from * to last tr group, 1tr in next ch sp, tr3tog over same ch sp, next ch sp and top of tr2tog from previous row.

Row 36: 1ch, 1dc in tr3tog from previous row, miss next tr, 1tr in next dc, *2ch, miss next 2 tr, 1dc in each of next 3 tr, 2ch, miss next 2 tr, 1tr in next dc; rep from * to last dc, 2ch, 1tr in last dc, 2ch, miss next tr, 1dc in top of first tr2tog from previous row.

Row 37: 3ch, 1tr in first 2-ch sp, 1ch, [1tr, 1ch] twice in next ch sp, *miss next 3dc **, [1tr, 1ch] twice in next ch sp, miss next tr, [1tr, 1ch] twice in next ch sp; rep from * ending last rep at **, 1tr in next ch sp, 1tr in first dc from previous row.

Row 38: *5ch, miss next ch sp, 1dc in next ch sp (centre of V-st); rep from * to last ch sp, miss last ch sp, 2ch, 1tr in top of first 3-ch from previous row.

Row 39: 3ch, miss first 2-ch sp, [tr2tog, 1tr] in first 5-ch sp, *2ch, 1dc in next 5-ch sp, 2ch, 3tr in next 5-ch sp; rep from * to end.

Row 40: 3ch, miss first 2 tr, 1tr in next tr, 1ch, *miss next [ch sp, dc, ch sp], [1tr, 1ch] in next tr (first of 3-tr group), [1tr, 1ch] twice in next tr (centre of 3-tr group), [1tr, 1ch] in next tr (last of 3-tr group); rep from * to last 3-tr group, 1tr in next tr, 1tr in top of tr2tog of previous row.

Row 41: 1ch, dc2tog over first 2 tr, *1dc in next ch sp, 2tr in next ch sp, 3tr in next ch sp, 2tr in next ch sp; rep from * to last ch sp, 1dc in next ch sp, dc2tog over same ch sp and top of first 3-ch from previous row.

Row 42 (WS): 3ch, miss dc2tog, dc and first 2tr, 1dc in each of next 3 tr, *miss next 2 tr, 2ch, 1tr in next dc, 2ch, miss next 2 tr, 1dc in each of next 3 tr: rep from * to end, miss last [2 tr, 1 dc], 1tr in top of dc2tog from previous row.

Fasten off.

Edging

Sides 1, 2 and 3

Row 1 (WS): Working on the WS, join yarn in corner at start of Row 1.
1ch, make 96dc evenly along first edge to first corner, 3dc in first corner, make 88dc evenly along next edge to second corner, 3dc in second corner, make 96dc evenly along next edge. Turn.

Row 2 (RS): 3ch, miss first st, 1tr in each st to first of 3 corner stitches, *miss first corner dc, 5tr (shell) in next corner dc, miss next corner dc, 1tr in each st to next corner; rep from * once more. (96 sts along first edge, 88 sts along second edge, 96 sts along third edge)

Cut yarn, do not fasten off.

Thread 111 beads onto yarn for the first beading row (see page 26 – RS method of beading).

Row 3 (WS): Join yarn, 1ch, 1dc in first st, *2ch, miss next 3 sts, [1tr(PB), 1ch] 3 times in next st placing bead in each treble only. 1ch, miss 3 sts, 1dc in next st **; rep from * to last 3 sts before corner shell, 1ch, miss next 2 sts, 1dc in next st,

Corner 1:
2ch, miss next 2 sts, [1tr(PB), 2ch] 3 times in next st (centre of shell) placing a bead in each tr only, 2ch, miss next 2 sts, 1dc in next st, 2ch, miss next 2 sts, 2ch, [1tr(PB), 1ch] 3 times in next st (centre of shell) placing a bead in each tr only, 2ch, miss next 3 sts, 1dc in next st; rep from * ending at ** before next corner shell.

Corner 2:
2ch, miss next 2 sts, [1tr(PB), 2ch] 3 times in next st (centre of shell) placing a bead in each tr only, 2ch, miss next 2 sts, 1dc in next st, *2ch, miss next 3 sts, [1tr(PB), 1ch] 3 times in next st (centre of shell) placing a bead in each tr only, 2ch, miss next 3 sts, 1dc in next st; rep from * to next corner.

Cut yarn, do not fasten off. Turn.

Thread 259 beads onto yarn for the second beading row (see page 26 – WS method of beading).

Row 4 (RS): Join yarn into loop on hook.

Side 1:
1ch, 1dc in same st, *miss next 2-ch sp, 1tr(PB) in next 1-ch sp, 6ch (PB on fifth of this 6-ch), ss in fifth ch from hook, 1tr(PB) in same 1-ch sp, 10ch (PB on seventh of this 10-ch), ss in ninth ch from hook, 1tr(PB) in next 1-ch sp, 6ch (PB on fifth of this 6-ch), ss in fifth ch, 1tr(PB) in same 1-ch sp, 1dc in next dc; rep from * to last dc before next corner**.

Corner:
1dc in last dc before corner, 2ch, miss next 2-ch sp, 1tr(PB) in next 2-ch sp, 6ch (PB on fifth of this 6-ch), ss in fifth ch from hook, 1tr(PB) in same 2-ch sp, 10ch (PB on seventh of this 10-ch), ss in ninth ch, 1tr(PB) in next 2-ch sp, 6ch (PB on fifth of this 6-ch), ss in fifth ch from hook, 1tr(PB) in same 2-ch sp, 2ch, 1dc in next dc; rep from * once more and then rep from * to ** once more, 1dc in last dc.

Fasten off.

Neck edging

Side 4:
Working on RS and underside of foundation chain, join yarn in first ch. 1ch, 1dc in same ch, *3ch, ss in third ch from hook (picot), 1dc in each of next 3 sts; rep from * to end.

Fasten off.

Finishing

Sew in ends and lightly press with a damp cloth.

Tip

When you are using this yarn, always wind skeins into a ball before crocheting.

chapter two
warm tones

urchin
neckwarmer

The ends of this neckwarmer are shaped like petals and it has a tie that fastens with a popper, as well as a flower embellishment.

Materials

Neckwarmer
Fyberspates Vivacious DK, 100% superwash merino wool DK yarn
115g (4oz) skeins, approx 230m (253yd) per skein:
1 x skein of 816 Crocus (purple) (MC)

Flower
Debbie Bliss Baby Cashmerino, 55% wool/ 33% acrylic/12% cashmere 4 ply yarn
50g (1¾oz) balls, approx 125m (137yd) per ball:
Scrap of 18 Citrus (green) (A)
Scrap of 101 Ecru (off white) (B)

3.5mm (US size E/4) crochet hook

1 x snap fastener

Yarn sewing needle

Finished measurement

Approx 10cm (4in) wide x 82cm (32½in) long

Tension

19 sts x 8 rows over a 10cm (4in) square, working trebles using a 3.5mm (US size E/4) hook and Fyberspates Vivacious DK.

Abbreviations

approx approximately
ch chain
ch sp chain space
dc double crochet
dtr double treble
htr half treble
rep repeat
RS right side
st(s) stitch(es)
ss slip stitch
tr treble
WS wrong side
yrh yarn round hook

Special abbreviations

3trCL (3 treble cluster): *yrh, insert hook in next st, yrh, pull yarn through, yrh, pull through 2 loops, rep from * twice more, yrh, pull yarn through all 4 loops on hook.
tr2tog (treble crochet 2 stitches together): yrh, insert hook where instructed, yrh, pull yarn through, yrh and pull yarn through first 2 loops on hook, yrh, insert hook in next st, yrh and pull yarn through, yrh and pull yarn through first 2 loops (3 loops on hook), yrh and pull yarn through all 3 loops to complete the tr2tog.

Neckwarmer

Row 1: Using MC, make 6ch, 1tr in fourth ch from hook (counts as 1tr), 1tr in each of next 2 ch. (4 sts)

Row 2: 3ch (counts as 1tr), 1tr in first st, 2tr in each of next 2 sts, 2tr in top of 3-ch. (8 sts)

Row 3: 3ch (counts as 1tr), 1tr in first st, 2tr in each st to end, 2tr in top of 3-ch. (16 sts)

Row 4: 3ch (counts as 1tr), 1tr in first st, 1tr in each st to end, 2tr in top of 3-ch. (18 sts)

Row 5: 3ch (counts as 1tr), 1tr in first st, 1tr in each st to end, 2tr in top of 3-ch. (20 sts)

Next row: 3ch (counts as 1tr), miss first st, [tr2tog] 7 times. (*8 sts*)

Next row: 3ch (counts as 1tr), miss first st, [tr2tog] 3 times. (*4 sts*)

Fasten off.

Press lightly with a damp cloth on WS.

Tie

Row 1: Using MC, make 9ch, 1tr in fourth ch from hook, 1tr in each of next 6 sts. (7 sts)

Row 2: 3ch (counts as 1tr), 1tr in each st to end. (7 sts)

Rep Row 2 until work measures 14cm (5½in) or 11 rows (enough rows to fit all the way around both ends of the scarf bunched up).

Fasten off, leaving a long tail for sewing onto scarf.

Flower

Using A, make 6ch, join with a ss to form a ring.

Round 1: 1ch, 12dc in ring, join with a ss in first dc.

Cut yarn, do not fasten off.

Round 2: Join B in loop on hook. 1ch, 1dc in same st, 1dc in next st, *3ch, 3trCL in same st, 3ch, 1dc in same st, 1dc in each of next 2 sts; rep from *, ending last rep with a ss in top of first dc. (6 petals)

Round 3: With RS facing but working into back stitches of the flower, 1ch, 1dc in back loops of first dc of previous round, *3ch, flip petal forwards, while keeping RS facing of rest of flower facing, 1dc in back loops of next dc from previous round (between petals); rep from * ending 3ch, join with a ss in first dc. (6 ch-sps)

Round 4: Working in ch sps from previous round, 1ch, *[1dc, 1htr, 1tr, 3dtr, 1tr, 1htr, 1dc] in next ch sp; rep from * in each ch sp to end, join with a ss in first 1-ch. (6 petals)

Fasten off.

Sew in ends, enclosing centre hole with yarn end.

Finishing

Sew one short end of tie on right side edge of work approx 19cm (7½in) from tip of left-hand end. Sew one side of snap fastener in centre of Tie end on same side and other side of snap fastener to match on other side of Tie end.

Sew Flower onto end of Tie on Right Side.

How to tie

Place scarf around neck with Flower tie on the under edge on the right-hand side.

Place the tie over the top of the left-hand side of scarf, keeping the popper at the front.

Wrap the tie underneath, past the left-hand side and the right-hand side of the scarf.

Bringing the flower round to the front and fasten the snap fastener.

Tip

When you are using this yarn, always wind skeins into a ball before crocheting.

Row 6: 3ch (counts as 1tr), 1tr in first st, 1tr in each st to end, 2tr in top of 3-ch. (22 sts)

Row 7: 3ch (counts as 1tr), miss first st, 1tr in each st to end. (21 sts)

Row 8: 3ch (counts as 1tr), 1tr in each st. (21 sts)

Row 9: 3ch (counts as 1tr), tr2tog over first 2 sts, 1tr in each st to last 2 sts, tr2tog over last 2 sts. (19 sts)

Row 10: 3ch (counts as 1tr), 1tr in first st, 1tr in each st to end, 1tr in top of 3-ch. (20 sts)

Row 11: 3ch (counts as 1tr), tr2tog, 1tr in each st to last st, tr2tog over last 2 sts. (18 sts)

Row 12: 3ch (counts as 1tr), 1tr in first st, 1tr in each st to end, 1tr in top of 3-ch. (19 sts)

Row 13: 3ch (counts as 1tr), miss first tr, 1tr in each st to end, 1tr in top of 3-ch. (19 sts)

Rep Row 13 until work measures approx 68cm (27¼in).

Next row: 3ch (counts as 1tr), miss first tr, 1tr in each st to end. (18 sts)

Next row: 3ch (counts as 1tr), 1tr in each st to end. (18 sts)

Next row: 3ch (counts as 1tr), 1tr in first st, 1tr in each st to end, 2tr in top of 3-ch. (20 sts)

Next row: 3ch (counts as 1tr), miss first tr, 1tr in each st to last st. (19 sts)

Next row: 3ch (counts as 1tr), 2tr in first st, 1tr in each st to end, 1tr in top of 3-ch. (21 sts)

Next row: 3ch (counts as 1tr), 1tr in each st to end. (21 sts)

Next row: 3ch (counts as 1tr), 1tr in first tr, 1tr in each st to end, 1tr in top of 3-ch. (22 sts)

Next row: 3ch (counts as 1tr), tr2tog, 1tr in each st to last 2 sts, tr2tog. (20 sts)

Next row: 3ch (counts as 1tr), tr2tog, 1tr in each st to last 2 sts, tr2tog. (18 sts)

Next row: 3ch (counts as 1tr), tr2tog, 1tr in each st to last 2 sts, tr2tog. (16 sts)

kiosk
scarf

Joined up flower motifs make a lovely delicate and unusual scarf. The colours remind me of seaside sweet shops and summer time in Brighton.

Materials

Louisa Harding Cassia, 75% superwash merino/25% nylon DK yarn
50g (1¾oz) balls, approx 133m (145yd) per ball:
4 x balls of 102 Ecru (off white) (MC)
1 x ball each of:
108 Lime (green) (A)
103 Chick (yellow) (B)
112 Prince (dark blue) (C)
105 Glacier (pale blue) (D)
104 Powder (pale pink) (E)
115 Lipstick (bright pink) (F)
111 Earth (dark brown) (G)
121 Mink (pale brown) (H)

3.5mm (US size E/4) crochet hook

Yarn sewing needle

Finished measurement

Approx 23cm (9in) wide x 184cm (72in) long

Tension

Each motif measures approx 14cm (5½in) tip to tip of petal, using a 3.5mm (US size E/4) hook and Louisa Harding Cassia.

Abbreviations

approx approximately
ch chain
ch sp chain space
dc double crochet
rep repeat
RS right side
ss slip stitch
tr treble
WS wrong side

Colourway

Make 28 motifs in total.
Always use MC for Rounds 3, 4, 5.
4 x Round 1: green (A), Round 2: yellow (B)
4 x Round 1: dark blue (C), Round 2: pale blue (D)
4 x Round 1: pale pink (E), Round 2: bright pink (F)
4 x Round 1: dark brown (G), Round 2: pale brown (H)
3 x Round 1: pale blue (D), Round 2: dark blue (C)
3 x Round 1: yellow (B), Round 2: green (A)
3 x Round 1: bright pink (F), Round 2: pale pink (E)
3 x Round 1: pale brown (H), Round 2: dark brown (G)

Flower motif

(make 28)

Work on RS throughout.

Using first colour, make 6ch, join with a ss in first ch to form a ring.

Round 1: 3ch (counts as 1tr), 1tr, [2ch, 2tr in ring] 5 times, 2ch, join with a ss in top of first 3-ch. (6 ch sps)

Fasten off.

Round 2: Join second colour in first ch sp, 5ch (counts as 1tr, 2ch), 1tr in same ch sp, 1ch, [1tr, 2ch, 1tr, 1ch in next ch sp] 5 times, join with a ss in third of first 5ch. (6 x 2-ch sps, 6 x 1-ch sps)

Fasten off.

Round 3: Join MC in first 2-ch sp, 3ch (counts as 1tr), [1tr, 2ch, 2tr] in same ch sp, 1dc in next 1-ch sp, *[2tr, 2ch, 2tr] in next 2-ch sp, 1dc in next 1-ch sp; rep from * 4 more times, join with a ss in top of first 3ch. (6 petals)

Round 4: Ss in first tr, ss in first ch sp, 3ch (counts as 1tr), [2tr, 3ch, 3tr] in same ch sp, *1tr in next tr, miss next tr, 1dc in next dc, miss next tr, 1tr in next tr, [3tr, 3ch, 3tr] in next ch sp; rep from * 4 times more, 1tr in next tr, miss next tr, 1dc in next dc, miss next tr, 1tr in first ss, join with a ss in top of first 3-ch. (6 petals)

Round 5: 3ch (counts as 1tr), 1tr in each of first 2tr, *[3tr, 3ch, 3tr] in next ch sp, 1tr in each of next 3tr, miss next tr, 1dc in next dc, miss next tr, 1tr in each of next 3tr; rep from * 4 times more, [3tr, 3ch, 3tr] in next ch sp, 1tr in each of next 3tr, miss next tr, 1dc in next dc, miss next tr, join with a ss in top of first 3-ch. (6 petals)

Fasten off.

Tip

Sew in ends after making each motif, closing the hole in the centre with the first end.

Finishing

Block and lightly press each motif on WS.

Lay out motifs in two lines, with colours evenly distributed and petal corners touching (see photo, right). Pin and sew petal corners together using a yarn sewing needle on WS. Sew in ends.

sunset
cowl

This is a really soft yarn, which makes this lovely cowl drape beautifully – and it's also very comfortable on the neck. The puff stitch creates an interesting texture.

Materials

Debbie Bliss Paloma, 60% baby alpaca/ 40% merino wool super chunky yarn 50g (1¾oz) balls, approx 65m (71yd) per ball: 2 x balls of 015 Ruby (red)

8mm (US size L/11) crochet hook

Yarn sewing needle

Finished measurement

Approx 61cm (24in) around x 22.5cm (9in) deep

Tension

7 rows x 9 sts over a 10cm (4in) square working Puff st using an 8mm (US size L/11) hook and Debbie Bliss Paloma.

Abbreviations

approx approximately
ch chain
ch sp chain space
htr half treble
rep repeat
RS right side
st(s) stitch(es
yrh yarn round hook)

Special abbreviation

Puff: yrh, insert hook where directed, yrh, pull yarn through, yrh, insert hook in same place, yrh, pull yarn through, yrh, insert hook in same place, yrh, pull yarn through (7 loops on hook), yrh, pull yarn through all 7 loops on hook.

Cowl

Row 1 (RS): Make 25ch, 1htr in third ch from hook (first 2 ch counts as 1htr), 1htr in each of next 2 ch, 1ch, *miss 1 ch, 1 Puff in next ch, 1ch, miss 1 ch, 1htr in each of next 4 ch, 1ch; rep from * once more, miss 1 ch, 1 Puff in next ch, 1ch, miss 1 ch, 1htr in each of last 3 ch.

Row 2: 2ch (counts as 1htr), miss first st, 1htr in each of next 2 sts, *1 Puff in next ch sp, 1ch, miss next Puff (from previous row), 1 Puff in next ch sp, 1htr in each of next 4 sts; rep from * once more, 1 Puff in next ch sp, 1ch, miss next Puff, 1 Puff in next ch sp, 1htr in each of last 2 sts, 1htr in top of first 2-ch from previous row.

Row 3: 2ch (counts as 1htr), miss first st, 1htr in each of next 2 sts, *1ch, miss next Puff, 1 Puff in next ch sp (between 2 Puffs from previous row), 1ch, miss next Puff, 1htr in each of next 4 sts; rep from * once more, 1ch, miss next Puff, 1 Puff in next ch sp (between 2 Puffs from previous row), 1ch, miss next Puff, 1htr in each of last 2 sts, 1htr in top of first 2-ch from previous row.

Rep Rows 2 and 3 until work measures approx 61cm (24in) ending on a Row 2. Fasten off.

Finishing

With RS together join seam. Turn right side out. To wear, slip over head, keeping seam at the back.

scarf

A lovely vintage-pink scarf, using Catherine Wheel stitch crocheted horizontally. It also has very pretty scalloped edging.

Materials

Debbie Bliss Rialto DK, 100% merino wool DK yarn

50g (1¾oz) balls, approx 105m (115yd) per ball: 4 x balls of 066 Vintage Pink (pink)

3.5mm (US size E/4) crochet hook

Yarn sewing needle

Finished measurement

Approx 15cm (6in) wide x 142cm (56in) long including edging

Tension

2 patts x 10 rows over a 9cm (3½in) square, using a 3.5mm (US size E/4) hook and Debbie Bliss Rialto DK.

Abbreviations

approx approximately
ch chain
ch sp chain space
dc double crochet
dtr double treble
rep repeat
RS right side
st(s) stitch(es)
tr treble
trtr triple treble
WS wrong side
yrh yarn round hook

Special abbreviations

3trCL (3 treble cluster): *yrh, insert hook in st or sp, yrh, pull yarn through, yrh, pull through 2 loops, rep from * twice more, yrh, pull yarn through all 4 loops on hook.

4trCL (4 treble cluster): *yrh, insert hook in st or sp, yrh, pull yarn through, yrh, pull through 2 loops, rep from * 3 times more, yrh, pull yarn through all 5 loops on hook.

7trCL (7 treble cluster): *yrh, insert hook in st or sp, yrh, pull yarn through, yrh, pull through 2 loops, rep from * 6 times more, yrh, pull yarn through all 8 loops on hook.

Scarf

Row 1: Make 307ch, 1dc in loop at back of 2nd ch from hook, 1dc in loop at back of next ch, *miss 3 ch, 7tr in loop at back of next ch, miss 3 ch, 1dc in each loop at back of next 3 ch; rep from * to last 4 ch, miss 3 ch, 4tr in loop at back of last ch.

Row 2 (RS): 1ch, 1dc in each of first 2 sts, *3ch, 7trCL over next 7 sts, 3ch, 1dc in each of next 3 sts; rep from * to last 4 sts, 3ch, 4trCL over last 4 sts.

Row 3: 3ch (counts as 1tr), 3tr in top of 4trCL, *miss 3 ch, 1dc in each of next 3 dc, miss 3 ch, 7tr in closing loop of next 7trCL; rep from * to end, finishing miss 3 ch, 1dc in each of last 2 dc.

Row 4: 2ch (counts as 1tr) miss first st, 3trCL over next 3 sts, *3ch, 1dc in each of next 3 sts, 3ch, 7trCL over next 7 sts; rep from * to end, finishing 3ch, 1dc in next st, 1dc in top of 3-ch from previous row.

Row 5: 1ch, 1dc in each of first 2 dc, *miss 3 ch, 7tr in closing loop of next

7trCL, miss 3 ch, 1dc in each of next 3 dc; rep from * to end, finishing miss 3 ch, 4tr in top of 2-ch from previous row.

Rep Rows 2–5 twice and then Rows 3–5 once more, ending with a Row 5.

Fasten off.

Edging

With WS facing, join yarn at one edge, make 1ch, 1dc in same place as joining st. Make 19dc evenly across to end. (20 sts)

Row 1: 5ch (counts as 1dtr, 1ch), [1dtr, 1ch] twice in first dc, miss 4 dc, 1dc in next dc, *1ch, miss 4 dc, [1dtr, 1ch in next dc] 5 times, miss 4 dc, 1dc in next dc, miss 3 dc, [1ch, 1dtr in last dc] 3 times.

Row 2: 1ch, 1dc in first dtr, *2ch, [1trtr, 2ch] 4 times in next dc, miss 2 dtr, 1dc in next dtr; rep from * once more, ending last dc in fourth of first 5-ch from previous row.

Row 3: 1ch, 1dc in first dc, *4ch, miss next ch sp, 3trCL in next 2-ch sp, [3ch, 3trCL in next 2-ch sp] twice, 4ch, 1dc in next dc; rep from * once more.

Fasten off.

Rep Edging at other end of scarf.

Finishing

Sew in ends.

Tip

Working into the loop at the back of the chain of the first row creates an edge that will be the same visually as the last row of the scarf. This method can also be used when there is no edging.

Landsdowne
chunky scarf

A great chunky scarf for the depths of winter, in a gorgeous crimson colour and worked using a lovely shell stitch.

Materials

Debbie Bliss Roma, 70% merino/30% alpaca super chunky yarn

100g (3½oz) balls, approx 80m (87yd) per ball:
3 x balls of 16 Crimson (red) (MC)
1 x ball of 10 Teal (blue-green) (A)

10mm (US size N/15) and 8mm (US size L/11) crochet hooks

Yarn sewing needle

Finished measurement

Approx 17.5cm (7in) wide x 162cm (64in) long (excluding tassels)

Tension

3 rows x 1½ pattern stitches over a 10cm (4in) square, using 10mm (US size N/15) hook and Debbie Bliss Roma.

Abbreviations

approx approximately
ch chain
ch sp chain space
dc double crochet
htr half treble
rep repeat
RS right side
sp space
st(s) stitch(es)
tr treble
WS wrong side
yrh yarn round hook

Special abbreviations

dc3tog (double crochet 3 stitches together): insert hook in next st, yrh, pull yarn through (2 loops on hook), insert hook in next st, yrh, pull yarn through (3 loops on hook), insert hook in next st, yrh, pull yarn through (4 loops on hook), yrh, pull yarn through all 4 loops on hook.
Shell: [3tr, 1ch, 3tr]
V-st: [1htr, 1ch, 1htr]

Scarf

Row 1: Using MC and 10mm (US size N/15) hook, make 22ch, 1dc in second ch from hook, 1dc in each ch to end. (21 sts)

Row 2: 1ch, 1dc in each of first 2 sts, *miss next 3 sts, [3tr, 1ch, 3tr] (Shell) in next st, miss next 3 sts, 1dc in next st, miss 1 st, 1ch, 1dc in next st, miss next 3 sts, [3tr, 1ch, 3tr] in next st, miss next 3 sts, 1dc in each of last 2 sts.

Row 3: 2ch, 1htr in first st, 3ch, 1dc in 1-ch sp (centre of next Shell), 3ch, [1htr, 1ch, 1htr] (V-st) in 1-ch sp (between 2-dc from previous Row), 3ch, 1dc in next 1-ch sp (centre of next Shell), 3ch, 2htr in last dc.

Row 4: 3ch, 3tr in first htr, 1dc in next 3-ch sp, 1ch, 1dc in next 3-ch sp, [3tr, 1ch, 3tr] in next 1-ch sp (centre of V-st from previous row), 1dc in next 3-ch sp, 1ch, 1dc in next 3-ch sp, 4tr in top of first 2-ch.

Row 5: 1ch, 1dc in first st, 3ch, [1htr, 1ch, 1htr] in next 1-ch sp between 2-dc of previous row, 3ch, 1dc in 1-ch sp (centre of next

Shell), 3ch, [1htr, 1ch, 1htr] in next 1-ch sp between 2dc of previous row, 3ch, 1dc in top of first 3-ch.

Row 6: 1ch, 1dc in first st, 1dc in first 3-ch sp, [3tr, 1ch, 3tr] in next V-st, 1dc in next 3-ch sp, 1ch, 1dc in next 3-ch sp, [3tr, 1ch, 3tr] in next V-st, 1dc in next 3-ch sp, 1dc in last dc.

Rep Rows 3–6 until work measures approx 162cm (64in) ending on a Row 3.

Edging side 1

Next row (RS): Working on RS, 1ch, 1dc in each of first 2htr, 3dc in next ch sp, 1dc in next st, 3dc in next ch sp, 3dc in next ch sp, 3dc in next ch sp, 1dc in next st, 3dc in next ch sp, 1dc in next st, 1dc in top of first 2-ch. (21 sts)

Change to 8mm (US size L/11) hook.

Next row (WS): 1ch, miss first st, 1dc in each of next 8 sts, dc3tog, 1dc in each of next 8 sts, miss last st. (17 sts)

Cut yarn, do not fasten off.

Next row (RS): Join A, 1ch, 1dc in each st to end. (17 sts)

Cut yarn, do not fasten off.

Next row (WS): Join MC, 1ch, 1dc in each st to end.

Fasten off.

Edging side 2

Row 1 (WS): Working on WS and underside of ch from Row 1, join MC in first ch, 1ch, miss next ch, 1dc in each of next 8 sts, dc3tog, 1dc in each of next 8ch, miss last st. (17 sts)

Cut yarn, do not fasten off.

Row 2 (RS): Join A, 1ch, 1dc in each st to end. (17 sts)

Cut yarn, do not fasten off.

Row 3 (WS): Join MC, 1ch, 1dc in each st to end.

Fasten off.

Finishing

Sew in ends.

Block and press scarf.

starfish
cowl

This is a great project for people who don't like to wear wool, because it's made using a 100% cotton tape yarn. It's worked using a chevron stitch and wraps around the neck twice.

Materials

Debbie Bliss Delphi, 100% cotton tape yarn 50g (1¾oz) balls, approx 50m (54yd) per ball: 6 x balls of 011 Peach

6mm (US size J/10) crochet hook

Yarn sewing needle

Finished measurement

Approx 22.5cm (9in) deep x 114cm (45in) around

Tension

5 rows of pattern x 15 sts of pattern rows over a 10cm (4in) square, using 6mm (US size J/10) hook and Debbie Bliss Delphi.

Abbreviations

approx approximately
ch chain
ch sp chain space
rep repeat
st(s) stitch(es)
tr treble

Cowl

Row 1: Make 32ch. 1tr in third ch from hook (counts as 2tr), 1tr in each of next 3 ch, *miss next 2 ch, 1tr in each of next 4 ch, 2ch, 1tr in each of next 4 ch; rep from * to last 6 ch, miss 2 ch, 1tr in each of next 3 ch, 2tr in last ch.

Row 2: 3ch (counts as 1tr), 1tr in first st, 1tr in each of next 3 sts, *miss 2 sts, 1tr in each of next 3 sts, [1tr, 2ch, 1tr] in next 2-ch sp, 1tr in each of next 3 sts; rep from * to last 6 sts, miss 2 sts, 1tr in each of next 3 sts, 2tr in top of first 3-ch.

Rep Row 2 until work measures approx 114cm (45in).

Fasten off.

Finishing

Pin and sew seam. Sew in ends. Turn right side out.

sunrise
cowl

Materials

Debbie Bliss Lara, 58% merino/42% superfine alpaca chunky/super chunky yarn
100g (3½oz) balls, approx 60m (65yd) per ball:
1 x ball each of:
09 Nadia (dark grey) (A)
01 Pasha (off white) (B)
04 Yuri (light grey) (C)
11 Amelia (orange) (D)

8mm (US size L/11) crochet hook

Yarn sewing needle

Finished measurement

Approx 24cm (9½in) deep x 150cm (60in) around

Tension

8 sts x 5 rows over a 10cm (4in) square working half trebles using an 8mm (US size L/11) hook and Debbie Bliss Lara.

Abbreviations

approx approximately
ch chain
htr half treble
rep repeat
st(s) stitch(es)

This is a really great scarf for wearing in the depths of winter. Even though the yarn is thick and chunky it's extra soft, so it feels comfortable and warm around the neck. It also crochets up really quickly using half trebles and can be made over a couple of evenings. I have put this at Level 2 – the stitch is really simple and great for a beginner, but the yarn is a little fluffy and it takes time to find the stitches.

Scarf

Row 1: Using A, make 21ch, 1htr in third ch from hook, 1htr in each ch to end. (19 sts)

Row 2: 2ch, 1htr in each st to end. (19 sts)

Row 3: Rep Row 2 until either the end of the ball has been reached (ending at the end of a row and not in the middle), or 19 rows have been worked or work measures approx 37.5cm (15in).

Change to B, rep Rows 2 and 3 for another 37.5cm (15in).

Change to C, rep Rows 2 and 3 for another 37.5cm (15in).

Change to D, rep Rows 2 and 3 for another 37.5cm (15in).

Fasten off.

Finishing

Join seam.

chapter three
natural and rustic

sunshower
scarf

This long chevron stitch striped scarf in contemporary colours makes a lovely fashion statement and keeps you warm at the same time.

Materials

Debbie Bliss Rialto DK, 100% merino wool DK yarn 50g (1¾oz) balls, approx 105m (115yd) per ball:
4 x balls of 004 Grey (A)
1 x ball each of:
001 White (B)
045 Gold (C)

3.5mm (US size E/4) crochet hook

Yarn sewing needle

Finished measurement

Approx 20cm (8in) wide x 233.5cm (92in) long

Tension

15 sts x 9 rows over a 10cm (4in) square, worked in treble crochet using a 3.5mm (US size E/4) hook and Debbie Bliss Rialto DK.

Abbreviations

approx approximately
ch chain
htr half treble
rep repeat
st(s) stitch(es)
tr treble

Colourway

Work in a repeating stripe sequence of 14 rows A, 14 rows B, 14 rows A, 14 rows C.

Scarf

Row 1: Using A, make 46ch. 2htr in second ch from hook, [1htr in each of next 4 ch, miss 2 ch, 1htr in each of next 4 ch, 3htr in next ch] 3 times, 1htr in each of next 4 ch, miss 2 ch, 1htr in each of next 4 ch, 2htr in last ch.

Row 2: 2ch, 2htr in first st, [1htr in each of next 4 sts, miss 2 sts, 1htr in each of next 4 sts, miss next 2 sts, 3htr in next st] 3 times, 1htr in each of next 4 sts, miss next 2 sts, 1htr in each of next 4 sts, 2htr in last st.

Rep Row 2 until 14 rows in A have been worked.

Cut yarn, do not fasten off.

Join B, continue to work Row 2 until another 14 rows have been worked.

Continue working in following sequence A, C, A, B (working 14 rows in each colour) until scarf measures approx 233.5cm (92in), ending last 14 rows using colour A.

Fasten off.

Finishing

Sew in ends.

Skill Rating
★ ★ ★ ★

sea salt
cowl

This cowl is very quick to make, in a beautiful soft yarn using a double crochet stitch – it's a great project that will take just an evening to finish. It really helps to use a stitch marker in the first chain of every round.

Materials

Debbie Bliss Lara, 58% merino/ 42% superfine alpaca chunky/super chunky yarn

100g (3½oz) balls, approx 60m (65yd) per ball:

1 x ball of 01 Pasha (off white)

10mm (US size N/15) crochet hook

Stitch marker

Yarn sewing needle

Finished measurement

Approx 30cm (12in) wide x 17.5cm (7in) long

Tension

6 sts x 8 rows over a 10cm (4in) square working double crochet using a 10mm (US size N/15) hook and Debbie Bliss Lara.

Abbreviations

approx approximately
ch chain
dc double crochet
rep repeat
st(s) stitch(es)
ss slip stitch

Cowl

Make 35ch, ss into first ch to form a circle, ensuring that the chain is not twisted.

Round 1: 1ch, (place a st marker) 1dc in each ch to end, ss in first dc. (35 sts)

Round 2: 1ch, (place st marker) 1dc in next st, 1dc in each st to end, ss in first dc. (35 sts)

Rep Round 2 until work measures approx 17.5cm (7in).

Fasten off.

Finishing

Sew in ends.

dune
cowl

This pretty shell stitch is one of my favourite stitches, and Baby Cashmerino is one of my favourite yarns – it's a lovely yarn to have close to the skin. Wear this cowl wrapped around the neck twice.

Materials

Debbie Bliss Baby Cashmerino, 55% wool/ 33% acrylic/12% cashmere 4 ply yarn 50g (1¾oz) balls, approx 125m (137yd) per ball: 4 x balls of 066 Amber (yellow)

4mm (US size E/4) crochet hook

Yarn sewing needle

Finished measurement

17.5cm (7in) deep x 145cm (52in) around

Tension

3 shell patterns and 12 rows over a 10cm (4in) square, using a 4mm (US size E/4) hook and Debbie Bliss Baby Cashmerino.

Abbreviations

approx approximately
ch chain
dc double crochet
rep repeat
st(s) stitch(es)
tr treble
WS wrong side

Cowl

Row 1: Make 254ch, 1dc in second ch from hook, 1dc in each ch to end. (253 sts)

Row 2: 1ch, 1dc in first ch, *miss 2 ch, 5tr in next ch (Shell made), miss 2 ch, 1dc in next ch; rep to end, ending 1dc in last ch.

Row 3: 3ch (counts as 1tr), 2tr in first dc, *miss 2 tr, 1dc in next tr (top of Shell), miss 2 tr, 5tr in next dc, rep from * to end, ending with 3tr in last dc.

Row 4: 1ch, 1dc in first tr, *miss 2 tr, 5tr in next dc, miss 2 tr, 1dc in next tr; rep from * to end, ending 1dc in top of 3-ch.

Rep Rows 3 and 4 until work measures approx 17.5cm (7in) ending with Row 4.

Fasten off.

Finishing

With WS facing, join seam. Sew in ends and turn right side out.

Wear wrapped around neck twice.

Tip

Mark every 10 or 20 stitches to keep count when making a long chain.

jewel
cowl

Using a silk yarn in jewel-like hues, this cowl is just perfect for wrapping around the neck. Warm but light, with splashes of colour in the centre of each square.

Materials

Fyberspates Scrumptious 4 ply Sport, 55% merino/ 45% silk 4 ply yarn

100g (3½oz) skeins, approx 365m (399yd) per skein:

2 x skeins of 318 Glisten (grey) (MC)

1 x skein each (A) of:

306 Baby Pink (pale pink)

302 Gold (gold)

311 Flying Saucer (pale green)

315 Magenta (deep pink)

304 Water (blue)

3.5mm (US size E/4) crochet hook

Yarn sewing needle

Finished measurement

Approx 17.5cm (7in) deep x 129.5cm (51in) around (when sewn together), approx 131.5cm (52½in) before seam is joined and after pressing

Tension

Each square measures approx 4.5cm (1¾–2in), using a 3.5mm (US size E/4) hook and Fyberspates Scrumptious 4 ply Sport.

Abbreviations

approx approximate
ch chain
cont continue
dc double crochet
foll following
htr half treble
rep repeat
RS right side
ss slip stitch
st(s) stitch(es)
tr treble

Colourway

Make a total of 112 squares in the foll colours (with MC always used in Rounds 2 and 3):

23 baby pink
22 gold
22 pale green
23 deep pink
22 blue

Square

Using A, make 4ch, join with ss to form a ring.

Round 1: 1ch, 12dc in ring, cut A, do not fasten off, join MC with ss in first dc. (12 sts)

Round 2: Cont with MC, 3ch (counts as first tr), 1tr in same st, 2tr in each st to end, join with ss in top of 3-ch. (24 sts)

Round 3: 3ch (counts as 1tr), 2tr in same st (first corner), 1htr in next st, 1dc in each of next 3 sts, 1htr in next st. *3tr in next st (second corner), 1htr in next st, 1dc in each of next 3 sts, 1htr in next st; rep from * twice more (four corners), join with ss in top of first 3-ch.

Fasten off.

Tip

Sew in ends after making each square. When sewing in end of Round 1, sew around the stitches and pull tight to close up the hole in the centre.

Finishing

Block and press squares lightly using a damp cloth.

Set out 112 squares with 28 squares along x 4 squares deep, with the colours evenly spaced and with squares wrong sides facing up.

With right sides together and MC, join squares in the sets of 4 (112 sets). Join these 112 sets together using MC and in the order set out.

Block and press lightly on the wrong side.

With right sides together, join seam. Turn right side out.

Edging

With RS facing, join MC in one stitch to the side of the seam. 1ch, 1dc in same st, 1dc in next and each st around top to end. Do not put a dc into the seam. Join with a ss into first dc.

Fasten off.

Rep for the bottom edge.

Tip

When you are using this yarn, always wind skeins into a ball before crocheting.

beach hut
scarf

Materials

Debbie Bliss Rialto DK, 100% merino wool DK yarn
50g (1¾oz) balls, approx 105m (115yd) per ball:
1 x ball each of:
072 Ocean (blue) (A)
012 Scarlet (red) (B)
066 Vintage Pink (pink) (C)
005 Chocolate (brown) (D)
044 Aqua (blue-green) (E)
002 Ecru (off-white) (F)
045 Gold (yellow) (G)

4mm (US size G/6) crochet hook

Yarn sewing needle

Finished measurement

Approx 12.5cm (5in) wide x 160cm (63in) long

Tension

25 sts x 21 rows over a 10cm (4in) square, working tweed
stitch using a 4mm (US size G/6) hook and Debbie Bliss
Rialto DK.

Abbreviations

approx approximately
ch chain
dc double crochet
rep repeat
st(s) stitch(es)
sp space

A really lovely stitch that shows off these bright colours well.
The tassels give the edges a bit of zing and swish.

Scarf

Row 1: Using A, make 34ch. 1dc in second ch from hook, 1dc in each ch
to end. (33 sts)

Cut yarn, do not fasten off.

Row 2: Join B, 1ch, 1dc into each of first 2 sts. *1ch, miss next st, 1dc in
next st; rep from * to last st, ending row with 1dc in last st.

Cut yarn, do not fasten off.

Row 3: Join C, 1ch, 1dc into first st, *1ch, 1dc into next ch sp; rep from *
to last 2 sts, 1ch, miss next st, 1dc in last st.

Cut yarn, do not fasten off.

Row 4: Join D, 1ch, 1dc into first st, 1dc in first ch sp, *1ch, 1dc into next
ch sp; rep from * to last st, 1dc in last dc.

Cut yarn, do not fasten off.

Rep Rows 3 and 4, using the following colour sequence E, F, G, A, B, C, D, until scarf measures approx 160cm (63in), ending with row using A.

Do not cut yarn.

Last row: 1ch, 1dc in each dc and in each ch sp to end.

Fasten off.

Finishing

Sew in ends.

Tassels

Using B, cut sixty 25.5cm (10in) lengths of yarn, to make 30 tassels in all (15 for each end of scarf). Fold two strands of yarn in half to make each tassel. Attach first tassel to first chain stitch at one end of scarf (see page 27), then attach one tassel in every alternate chain stitch, ending with one tassel in the end chain stitch.

Attach remaining 15 tassels to other end of scarf.

Andre
neckwarmer

Materials
Bergère de France Abakan, 68% synthetic/
32% polyester chunky yarn
50g (1¾oz) balls, approx 42m (45yd) per ball:
3 x balls of 34253 Marron (brown)

6mm (US size J/10) crochet hook

Yarn sewing needle

Finished measurement
Approx 22.5cm (9in) deep x 55.5cm (22in)
around

Tension
Not applicable to this project, since it is
impossible to see the stitches and rows
with this type of yarn.

Abbreviations
approx approximately
ch chain
rep repeat
RS right side
st(s) stitch(es)
ss slip stitch
tr treble
WS wrong side

This is made using an eyelash yarn, which is very fluffy and has long pieces of fibre so it can be difficult to see the stitches. I recommend that you only tackle this if you are an experienced crocheter – not because the stitch is difficult (it only uses trebles), but because you have to instinctively know where the stitches are. Once you get going, it will be a really fun and quick project to make.

Neckwarmer

Row 1: Make 21ch, 1tr in fourth ch from hook, 1tr in each ch to end. (20 sts)

Row 2: 3ch, 1tr in each st to end. (20 sts)

Rep Row 2 until work measures approx 55cm (22in).

Fasten off.

Finishing
Join seam.

sea spray
scarf

This is worked in a delicate stitch using a luxurious silk-mix yarn. The edgings have four rows of beading – see page 25 for tips on how to thread beads onto yarn and how to bead using double crochet and treble stitches.

Materials

Fyberspates Scrumptious DK, 55% merino wool/45% silk DK yarn
100g (3½oz) skeins, approx 220m (240yd) per skein:
3 x skeins of 110 Natural (cream)

Approx 124 x white seed beads, size 6

3.5mm (US size E/4) crochet hook

Yarn sewing needle

Finished measurement

Approx 16.5cm (6½in) wide x 190cm (75in) long

Tension

4 shell rows x 4 shells over a 10cm (4in) square, using a 3.5mm (US size E/4) hook and Fyberspates Scrumptious DK.

Abbreviations

approx approximately
ch chain
ch sp chain space
dc double crochet
rep repeat
RS right side
ss slip stitch
st(s) stitch(es)
sp space
tr treble
WS wrong side

Special abbreviations

V-st: [1tr, 3ch, 1tr]
2trCL (2 treble cluster): *yrh, insert hook in st or sp, yrh, pull yarn through, yrh, pull through 2 loops, rep from * once more, yrh, pull yarn through all 3 loops on hook.
PB: place bead following beading techniques for WS rows (see page 26).

Scarf

Make 45ch.

Row 1: 7tr in 10th ch from hook (Shell), *1ch, miss 4 ch, [1tr, 1ch] in next ch, miss 4 ch, 7tr in next ch; rep from * to last 5 ch, 1ch, 1tr in last ch.

Row 2: 4ch, 1tr in first tr, *1ch, miss next 2 tr (of Shell), 1tr in each of next 3 tr, 1ch, miss next ch sp, [1tr, 3ch, 1tr] (V-st) in top of next 1tr; rep from * to last ch sp, 1ch, [1tr, 1ch, 1tr] in last ch sp.

Row 3: 3ch, 3tr in first ch sp, *1ch, miss next ch sp, [1tr, 1ch] in second tr of next 3-tr group (centre st) **, miss next 1ch sp, 7tr in next 3-ch sp (centre of V-st); rep from * ending last rep at **, miss next ch sp, 1ch, 4tr in last ch sp.

Row 4: 3ch, miss first tr, 1tr in next tr, 1ch, miss next 2 tr and next ch sp, [1tr, 3ch, 1tr] (V-st) in next tr, *1ch, miss next ch sp and next 2 tr, 1tr in each of next 3 tr, 1ch, miss next 2 tr and next ch sp, [1tr, 3ch, 1tr] (V-st) in next tr; rep from * to last 3 tr, miss next 2 tr, 1tr in last tr, 1tr in top of first 3-ch.

Row 5: 4ch, miss first ch sp, *7tr in next 3-ch sp (centre of V-st), 1ch, miss next ch sp, [1tr, 1ch] in second tr of next 3-tr group (centre st), miss next ch sp; rep from * to last V-st, 7tr in next 3-ch sp (centre of V-st), miss last ch sp, 1ch, 1tr in top of first 3-ch.

Rep Rows 2–5 until Scarf measures approx 181.5cm (71½in) ending on a Row 5.

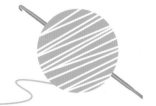

Fasten off.

Thread 62 beads on yarn for first edging.

Edging side 1:

Row 1 (beading row, WS): 4ch (PB on third of this 4-ch), 1tr(PB) in first tr, miss next ch sp, miss next 3 tr, *[2trCL in next tr, 3ch (PB in second of this 3-ch), 2trCL in same tr (middle of Shell)], miss next 3 tr, miss next ch sp,** [1tr(PB) in next tr, 3ch (PB in second of this 3-ch), 1tr (PB)] in same tr, miss next ch sp, miss next 3 tr; rep from * ending last rep at **, [1tr(PB), 1ch, 1tr(PB)] in last ch sp.

Row 2 (RS): 4ch, 1tr in first 1ch sp, *[2trCL, 3ch, 2trCL] in next 3-ch sp, ** (keeping the bead in between the clusters), [1tr, 3ch, 1tr] in next 3-ch sp (keeping the bead in between the trebles); rep from * ending last rep at **, [1tr, 1ch, 1tr] in last ch sp.

Row 3 (beading row, WS): 1ch, 1dc (PB) in first tr, 2ch, *[5tr(PB), 2ch] in next 3-ch sp (between clusters, placing a bead in each tr)**, [1dc(PB), 2ch] in next 3-ch sp (between trebles); rep from * ending last rep at **, 1dc(PB) in last ch sp.

Row 4 (beading row, RS): 1ss in first dc, 1ch, *[1dc in next tr, 3ch (PB on third of these ch), ss in first of 3-ch,] ss in same dc; rep from * 4 times more **. 1ch, 1dc in next dc, 1ch; rep from * three times more ending last rep at **, 1ch, ss in last dc.

Fasten off.

Thread 62 beads on yarn for second edging.

Edging side 2:

Working on underside of first 45ch at other end of Scarf with WS facing, join yarn in first ch sp.

Row 1 (WS): 4ch (PB on third of this 4-ch), 1tr(PB) in same sp, *[2trCL in bottom sp of 7-tr Shell, 3ch (PB in second of this 3-ch), 2trCL in same sp]**, [1tr (PB) in bottom of next 1-tr, 3ch (PB in second of this 3-ch), 1tr (PB] in same tr; rep from *, ending last rep at **, 1tr(PB) in 4th of first 10-ch from Row 1 of Scarf, 1ch, 1tr(PB) in same place.

Rep Rows 2–4 of Edging Side 1.

Fasten off.

Finishing
Sew in ends.

Tip
When you are using this yarn, always wind skeins into a ball before crocheting.

marina
scarf

Crocheting motifs is very satisfying, and triangles are a little more unusual. The triangle motifs on this scarf have a colourful flower centre, which really zings out against the pale grey.

Materials

Debbie Bliss Cashmerino Aran, 55% wool/ 33% acrylic/12% cashmere Aran yarn 50g (1¾oz) balls, approx 90m (98yd) per ball:
4 x balls of 27 Stone (pale grey) (MC)
1 x ball each of:
47 Aqua (blue) (A)
68 Hot Pink (bright pink) (B)
603 Baby Pink (pale pink) (C)
76 Willow (green) (D)

5mm (US size H/8) crochet hook

Yarn sewing needle

Finished measurement

Approx 17cm (7in) wide x 160cm (63in) long

Tension

Sides of each triangle measure approx 17.5cm (7in), using a 5mm (US size H/8) crochet hook and Debbie Bliss Cashmerino Aran.

Abbreviations

approx approximately
ch chain
ch sp chain space
col colour
dc double crochet
dtr double treble
rep repeat
RS right side
sp space
st(s) stitch(es)
ss slip stitch
tr treble
WS wrong side
yrh yarn round hook

Special abbreviations

frdc (front raised dc): insert hook from front, work 1dc around post of stitch.
dtr3CL (double treble cluster): *yrh 2 times, insert hook in st/sp, yrh, pull yarn through work, yrh, pull yarn through two loops on hook, yrh, pull yarn through two loops on hook; rep from * twice more (4 loops on hook), yrh, pull yarn through all 4 loops.

Colourway

Make a total of 16 triangles.
Always use MC for Rounds 3, 4, 5.
1 x Round 1: blue (A), Round 2: bright pink (B)
1 x Round 1: blue (A), Round 2: pale pink (C)
2 x Round 1: blue (A), Round 2: green (D)
2 x Round 1: bright pink (B), Round 2: blue (A)
1 x Round 1: bright pink (B), Round 2: pale pink (C)
1 x Round 1: bright pink (B), Round 2: green (D)
1 x Round 1: pale pink (C), Round 2: blue (A)
2 x Round 1: pale pink (C), Round 2: bright pink (B)
1 x Round 1: pale pink (C), Round 2: green (D)
1 x Round 1: green (D), Round 2: blue (A)
1 x Round 1: green (D), Round 2: bright pink (B)
2 x Round 1: green (D), Round 2: pale pink (C)

Triangle motif

(make 16)

Using first col, make 4ch, join to form a ring with ss in first ch.

Round 1: 5ch, [1tr, 2ch] in ring, 5 times, ss in third of 5-ch.

Fasten off first col.

Round 2: Join in second col in any 2-ch sp, *4ch, dtr3tog in next 2-ch sp, 4ch, 1 frdc around next tr from previous round; rep from * 5 more times, join with ss in same sp as joining st.
Fasten off second col.

Round 3: Join MC in top of any dtr3tog st from previous round.
6ch (counts as 1tr and 3ch), 1tr in same st, (corner) *3ch, 1dtr in next frdc, 3ch, 1dc in next dtr3tog, 3ch, 1dtr in next frdc, 3ch, ** [1tr, 3ch, 1tr] (corner) in next dtr3tog; rep from * once more, 3ch, 1dtr in next frdc, 3ch, 1dc in next dtr3tog, 3ch, 1dtr in next frdc, 3ch, join with ss in 3rd of first 6-ch.

Round 4: Ss in next 3-ch sp, 3ch (counts as 1tr), [1tr, 3ch, 2tr] in same ch sp (corner), * [1tr in next st, 3tr in next ch sp] 4 times, [2tr, 3ch, 2tr] in corner sp; rep from * to end, join with ss in top of first 3-ch. (21 tr on each side of triangle)

Round 5: Ss in first tr, ss in next ch sp, 3ch (counts as 1tr), [1tr, 3ch, 2tr] in same ch sp (corner), * 1tr in each st to next corner sp, [2tr, 3ch, 2tr] in corner sp; rep from * to end, join with ss in top of first 3-ch. (25 tr on each side of triangle)

Fasten off.

Finishing

With RS together and using a yarn sewing needle and MC, sew 16 triangles together using the photo to the left as a guide, making sure you alternate the colours of the flowers at the centre.

Edging

With RS facing, join MC in 3-ch sp in tip of one end, 1ch, 3dc in same ch sp,
*1dc in each of next 25 sts, (to join)
1dc in each of next 3 sps; rep from * to next tip of scarf, 3dc in ch sp; rep from * to end, join with ss in first dc.

Block and lightly press scarf on WS.

seaford
scarf

This is a very easy stitch, but it takes some concentration because the stitches are hard to see. The yarn is thick and soft and, even though it's a wide scarf, it scrunches around the neck very cosily.

Materials

Debbie Bliss Lara, 58% merino/42% superfine alpaca chunky/super chunky yarn
100g (3½oz) balls, approx 60m (65yd) per ball:
6 x balls of 01 Pasha (off white)

10mm (US size N/15) crochet hook

Yarn sewing needle

Finished measurement

Approx 26.5cm (10½in) wide x 229cm (90in) long including edging.

Tension

7 sts x 7 rows over a 10cm (4in) square working double crochet using a 10mm (US size N/15) hook and Debbie Bliss Lara.

Abbreviations

approx approximately
ch chain
dc double crochet
rep repeat
st(s) stitch(es)
ss slip stitch
tr treble

Special abbreviation

3trCL (3 treble cluster): *yrh, insert hook in st/sp, yrh, pull yarn through, yrh, pull through 2 loops, rep from * twice more, yrh, pull yarn through all 4 loops on hook.

Scarf

Row 1: Make 18ch, 1dc in second ch from hook, 1dc in each ch to end. (17 sts)

Row 2: 1ch, 1dc in each st to end. (17 sts)
Rep Row 2 until work measures approx 218cm (86in).
Do not fasten off.
Turn work and start next row of edging along last row worked of scarf.

Edging side 1:
*6ch, 3trCL in third ch from hook, ss in next ch, 2ch, miss 1 st, 1dc in next st; rep from * to end. (8 x 3trCLs)

Fasten off.

Edging side 2:
Join yarn in first ch of Row 1 and rep from * of Edging Side 1.

Fasten off.

Finishing

Sew in ends.

Brighton pier
chunky scarf

Materials

Debbie Bliss Cashmerino Aran, 55% wool/
33% acrylic/12% cashmere Aran yarn
50g (1¾oz) balls, approx 90m (98yd) per ball:
3 x balls of 09 Grey (MC)
2 x balls of 101 Ecru (A)
1 x ball of each of:
75 Citrus (yellow)
603 Baby Pink (pale pink)
72 Peach (pale orange)
48 Burnt Orange (orange)
47 Aqua (mid blue)
81 Mint (pale green)
61 Jade (bright green)
62 Kingfisher (bright blue)
56 Mallard (dark blue)
73 Coral (mid orange)

4.5mm (US size 7) crochet hook

Yarn sewing needle

Finished measurement

Approx 26.5cm (10½in) wide x 217cm (85½in)
long

Tension

Each square measures approx 12.5cm (5in),
using a 4.5mm (US size 7) hook and Debbie
Bliss Cashmerino Aran.

Abbreviations

approx approximately
ch chain
ch sp chain space
col colour
cont continue
dc double crochet
rep repeat
RS right side
ss slip stitch
tog together
tr treble

Colourway

Make a total of 30 squares. Always use A for
Round 4 and MC for Round 5, with a mixture of
other colours for Rounds 1–3.

When I decided to design a scarf using motifs, I searched high
and low for different square motif designs that would show off
this lovely Aran yarn. I made lots of samples, but the one I kept
coming back to was the traditional granny square. It's so simple
and stylish and this is the perfect project for a beginner.

Square

Work on RS throughout.

Using first col, make 4ch, join with ss in first ch to form a ring.

Round 1 (RS): Cont with first col, 3ch (counts as first tr), 2tr, 2ch in ring, [3tr, 2ch
in ring] 3 times. Join with ss in third of first 3-ch. (4 x 3tr groups)

Fasten off first col.

Round 2: Join second col with ss in any 2-ch, 3ch (counts as first tr), [2tr, 2ch, 3tr] in same 2-ch sp (corner), *1ch, [3tr, 2ch, 3tr] in next ch sp; rep from * twice more, 1ch, join with ss in third of first 3-ch. (4 corners)

Fasten off second col.

Round 3: Join third col with ss in any corner 2-ch sp, 3ch (counts as first tr), [2tr, 2ch, 3tr] in same 2-ch sp. *1ch, 3tr in next 1-ch sp, 1ch, [3tr, 2ch, 3tr] in next 2-ch sp; rep from * twice more, 1ch, 3tr in next 1-ch sp, 1ch, join with ss in third of first 3-ch.

Fasten off third col.

Round 4: Join A with ss in any corner 2-ch sp, 3ch (counts as first tr), [2tr, 2ch, 3tr] in same 2-ch sp, *[1ch, 3tr in next 1-ch sp] twice, 1ch, [3tr, 2ch, 3tr] in next 2-ch sp; rep from * twice more, [1ch, 3tr in next 1-ch sp] twice, 1ch, join with ss in third of first 3-ch. Fasten off A.

Round 5: Join MC with ss in any corner 2-ch sp, 3ch (counts as first tr), [2tr, 2ch, 3tr] in same 2-ch sp. *[1ch, 3tr in next 1-ch sp] three times, 1ch, [3tr, 2ch, 3tr] in next 2-ch sp; rep from * twice more, [1ch, 3tr in next 1-ch sp] three times, 1ch, join with ss in third of first 3-ch.

Fasten off.

Finishing

Sew in ends.

Arrange 2 squares wide x 15 squares long.

Using MC and WS tog, join seams up centre length, and then across each width.

After seams are joined, join yarn on RS of work at one end, 1ch, make 1dc in each st along end of scarf.

Fasten off.

Rep at other end of scarf.

Tip

If you don't feel like sewing in ends after each square, then at least sew in after two or three.

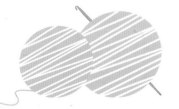
West pier
waves

Materials

Debbie Bliss Baby Cashmerino, 55% wool/
33% acrylic/12% cashmere 4 ply yarn
50g (1¾oz) balls, approx 125m (137yd)
per ball:

1 x ball of 66 Amber (yellow) (A)
4 x balls of 12 Silver (off white) (B)

444 x white seed beads, size 6

3.5mm (US size E/4) crochet hook

Yarn sewing needle

Finished measurement

approx 18cm (7in) wide x 170cm (67in) long

Tension

24 pattern stitches x 8 pattern rows over a
10cm (4in) square, using 3.5mm (US size E/4)
hook and Debbie Bliss Baby Cashmerino.

Abbreviations

approx approximately
ch chain
rep repeat
RS right side
st(s) stitch(es)
tr treble
WS wrong side

Special abbreviation

PB: place bead following beading techniques
for RS or WS rows (see page 26).

The beads on the tips of this scarf look like the white horses on the waves of the splashing sea… well at least near where I live. These little pearl beads give a lovely delicate edge to this understated scarf. This is also a really good project for learning how to bead on the right side and the wrong side using a treble stitch.

Scarf

Thread 222 beads onto yarn A. Bead in each st of next 7 beading rows, omitting placing a bead in the last tr of each row and the first 3ch.

Using A, make 38ch (without beads).

Row 1 (WS): PB in each tr, following WS beading method (see page 26) 1tr in fourth ch from hook (counts as first 3 ch), 1tr in each of next 2 ch, 3tr in next ch, 1tr in each of next 3 ch, *miss next 2 ch, 1tr in each of next 3 ch, 3tr in next ch, 1tr in each of next 3 ch; rep from * to last ch, 1tr in last ch (omitting bead in this last tr).

Row 2 (RS): PB in each tr, following RS beading method (see page 26). 3ch, miss first 2 sts, 1tr in each of next 3 sts, 3tr in next st (centre st of 3-tr group), 1tr in each of next 3 sts, *miss next 2 sts, 1tr in each of next 3 sts, 3tr in next st, 1tr in each of next 3 sts; rep from * to last st, miss last st, 1tr in top of 3-ch from previous row.

Rows 3–5: Rep Row 2, PB in each stitch, following beading techniques for RS rows and WS rows accordingly.

Row 6 (RS): Rep Row 2 with no beading.

Row 7 (WS): Rep Row 2, PB in each stitch, following WS beading method.

Cut yarn, do not fasten off.

Row 8 (RS): Join B, rep Row 2 without beading until work measures approx 152cm (60in) ending on a RS row.

Cut yarn, do not fasten off.

Thread 222 beads onto yarn B. PB in each st of next 7 beading rows, omitting placing a bead in the last tr of each row.

Next row (WS): Rep Row 2, following WS beading method.

Next row (RS): Rep Row 2 without beading.

Next 5 rows: Rep Row 2, following RS or WS beading method accordingly.

Fasten off.

Finishing

Sew in ends.

Tip

It's best to only thread on enough beads for the first seven rows at the start, and then thread on the beads for the last seven rows after the section using yarn B is finished. If you thread too many beads onto the yarn, it can shred and split with their weight.

chapter four
bold and bright

carousel
scarf

This beautiful shell stitch scarf is made with zingy sorbet shades, which are worked in big, bold blocks of colour.

Materials

Debbie Bliss Baby Cashmerino, 55% wool/
33% acrylic/12% cashmere 4 ply yarn
50g (1¾oz) balls, approx 125m (137yd) per ball:
2 x balls of 67 Sienna (orange) (A)
3 x balls of 68 Peach Melba (peach) (B)
2 x balls of 91 Acid Yellow (yellow) (C)

3.5mm (US size E/4) crochet hook

Yarn sewing needle

Finished measurement

Approx 18cm (7in) wide x 178cm (70in) long

Tension

3 shell rows x 3.5 shells over a 10cm (4in) square,
using a 3.5mm (US size E/4) hook and Debbie
Bliss Baby Cashmerino.

Abbreviations

approx approximately
ch chain
ch sp chain space
cont continue
dc double crochet
rep repeat
RS right side
st(s) stitch(es)
ss slip stitch
tr treble
WS wrong side
yrh yarn round hook

Special abbreviation

**tr2tog (treble crochet 2 stitches
together):** yrh, insert hook where instructed,
yrh, pull yarn through, yrh and pull yarn through
first 2 loops on hook, yrh, insert hook in next st,
yrh and pull yarn through, yrh and pull yarn through
first 2 loops (3 loops on hook), yrh and pull yarn
through all 3 loops to complete the tr2tog.

Scarf

Bottom edging:
Foundation row (RS): Using A, make 42ch, 1dc in
second ch from hook, 1dc in each ch to end. (41 sts)
Commence shell pattern:
Row 1 (RS): 1ch, 1dc in first st, *miss next 3 sts, 9tr in
next st (Shell), miss next 3 sts, 1dc in next st; rep from *
ending last repeat 1dc in first 1-ch from previous row.
Row 2: 3ch, 1tr in first dc, *5ch, miss next Shell, [1tr, 1ch,
1tr] in next dc; rep from * to last Shell, 5ch, miss last Shell,
2tr in last dc.

Row 3: 3ch, 4tr in first tr, *1dc in fifth tr of Shell from Row 1, (incorporating 5-ch from Row 2), 9tr in next 1-ch sp (between [1tr, 1ch, 1tr], from previous row); rep from * to last Shell, 1dc in fifth tr of Shell from Row 1, (incorporating 5-ch from Row 2), 5tr in top of first 3-ch from previous row.

Row 4: 3ch, miss first 5tr, [1tr, 1ch, 1tr] in next dc, *5ch, miss next Shell, [1tr, 1ch, 1tr] in next dc; rep from * to last Shell, 3ch, ss in top of first 3-ch from previous row.

Row 5: 1ch, 1dc over ss into first st of row below, *9tr in next 1-ch sp between [1tr, 1ch, 1tr] from previous row, 1dc in fifth tr of Shell from Row 3, (incorporating 5-ch from Row 2); rep from * ending last repeat 1dc in first of 3-ch from previous row.

Rep 2nd, 3rd, 4th and 5th rows of pattern, until work in A measures approx 44.5cm (17½in), ending on a Row 5.

Cut yarn, do not fasten off.

Join B, rep Rows 2, 3, 4 and 5 rows for approx 89cm (35in) of B, ending on a Row 5.

Cut yarn, do not fasten off.

Join C, rep Rows 2, 3, 4 and 5 for approx 44.5cm (17½in) in C.

Do not fasten off or cut yarn.

Bottom edging:
Next row: Cont with C, 1ch, 1dc in same st, miss next tr, *1dc in each of next 7 tr, miss 1 tr, tr2tog over last tr of next Shell and first tr of next Shell (miss the dc in between Shells); rep from * to last Shell, 1dc in each of next 7 tr, miss last tr, 1dc in last st. (41 sts)

Next row: Ss in each st to end.

Fasten off.

Finishing

Sew in ends.

helter skelter
scarf

A long skinny scarf that really shows off the gorgeous colours in this yarn range, which go with everything. The yarn has some cashmere fibres in it, to make it really soft!

Materials

Debbie Bliss Baby Cashmerino, 55% wool/33% acrylic/12% cashmere 4 ply yarn

50g (1¾oz) balls, approx 125m (137yd) per ball:

1 x ball each of:

99 Sea Green (green) (A)
89 Sapphire (bright blue) (B)
68 Peach Melba (peach) (C)
12 Silver (pale grey) (D)
91 Acid Yellow (yellow) (E)
93 Clematis (pale purple) (F)
204 Baby Blue (pale blue) (G)
101 Ecru (off-white) (H)

4mm (US size G/6) crochet hook

Yarn sewing needle

Finished measurement

Approx 11.5cm (4½in) wide x 239cm (94in) long

Tension

20 sts x 20 rows over a 10cm (4in) square, working double crochet using a 4mm (US size G/6) hook and Debbie Bliss Baby Cashmerino.

Abbreviations

approx approximately
ch chain
dc double crochet
rep repeat
st(s) stitch(es)

Scarf

Row 1: Using B, make 23ch, 1dc in second ch from hook, 1dc in each ch to end. (22 sts)

Rows 2–4: 1ch, 1dc in each st to end. (22 sts)
Cut yarn, do not fasten off.

Next 4 rows: Join A, rep Row 2. Cut yarn, do not fasten off.

Next 4 rows: Join G, rep Row 2. Cut yarn, do not fasten off.

Next 32 rows: Join C, rep Row 2. Cut yarn, do not fasten off.

Next 32 rows: Join E, rep Row 2. Cut yarn, do not fasten off.

Next 4 rows: Join F, rep Row 2. Cut yarn, do not fasten off.

Next 4 rows: Join H, rep Row 2. Cut yarn, do not fasten off.

Next 4 rows: Join A, rep Row 2. Cut yarn, do not fasten off.

Next 32 rows: Join B, rep Row 2. Cut yarn, do not fasten off.

Next 32 rows: Join G, rep Row 2. Cut yarn, do not fasten off.

Next 4 rows: Join C, rep Row 2. Cut yarn, do not fasten off.

Next 4 rows: Join E, rep Row 2. Cut yarn, do not fasten off.

Next 4 rows: Join H, rep Row 2. Cut yarn, do not fasten off.

Next 64 rows: Join D, rep Row 2. Cut yarn, do not fasten off.

Next 64 rows: Join H, rep Row 2. Cut yarn, do not fasten off.

Next 4 rows: Join G, rep Row 2. Cut yarn, do not fasten off.

Next 4 rows: Join B, rep Row 2. Cut yarn, do not fasten off.

Next 4 rows: Join E, rep Row 2. Cut yarn, do not fasten off.

Next 32 rows: Join C, rep Row 2. Cut yarn, do not fasten off.

Next 32 rows: Join G, rep Row 2. Cut yarn, do not fasten off.

Next 4 rows: Join A, rep Row 2. Cut yarn, do not fasten off.

Next 4 rows: Join D, rep Row 2. Cut yarn, do not fasten off.

Next 4 rows: Join F, rep Row 2. Cut yarn, do not fasten off.

Next 32 rows: Join E, rep Row 2. Cut yarn, do not fasten off.

Next 32 rows: Join D, rep Row 2. Cut yarn, do not fasten off.

Next 4 rows: Join C, rep Row 2. Cut yarn, do not fasten off.

Next 4 rows: Join B, rep Row 2. Cut yarn, do not fasten off.

Next 4 rows: Join A, rep Row 2. Fasten off.

Finishing
Sew in ends.

Hove
scarf

Materials

Fyberspates Scrumptious 4 ply Sport, 55% merino/45% silk 4 ply yarn 100g (3½oz) skeins, approx 365m (399yd) per skein:

1 x skein of 317 Denim (dark blue)

3.5mm (US size E/4) crochet hook

Approx 4.5m (5yd) of orange pompom trim (or enough to go right around scarf)

Yarn sewing needle

Finished measurement

Approx 21.5cm (8½in) wide x 183cm (72in) long

Tension

Approx 8 pattern rows x 6 pattern spaces over a 10cm (4in) square, using 3.5mm (US size E/4) hook and Fyberspates Scrumptious 4 ply Sport.

Abbreviations

approx approximately
ch chain
ch sp chain space
dc double crochet
RS right side
st(s) stitch(es)
sp space
ss slip stitch

The inspiration for this scarf came from wandering the quirky and fashionable streets of Hove, and seeing the popularity of blue and orange combinations. Pompoms are hard to resist, and this simple scarf – made using chain stitches – looks really stunning with a hand-sewn pompom trim edging.

Scarf

Make 54ch.

Row 1: 1dc in 6th ch from hook, *5ch, miss 3 ch, 1dc in next ch; rep from * ending last repeat 1dc in last ch. (13 x 5-ch sps)

Row 2: *5ch, 1dc in next 5-ch sp; rep from * to end of row. (13 x 5-ch sps)

Rep Row 2 until work measures approx 170cm (67in).

Do not fasten off.

Edging

First length: 1ch, [2dc in first sp, 2dc in 3rd of 5-ch, 2dc] in same corner sp (first corner), 4dc in next and each space down first side to next corner.

First width: *[2dc in corner sp, 2dc in 3rd of 5-ch, 2dc] in same corner sp, 4dc in each sp to next corner *.

Second length: Rep First width from * to *.

Second width: Rep First width from * to *. Join with ss in first dc.

Fasten off.

Finishing

Sew in ends.

Pin and hand sew bobble trim around RS of all edges.

Tip

When you are using this yarn, always wind skeins into a ball before crocheting.

North Laines
scarf

This is a delightful scarf to cheer up a winter's day. The yarn is lovely and soft and the colourful stripes will go with any outfit.

Materials
Louisa Harding Cassia, 75% superwash merino/25% nylon DK yarn
50g (1¾oz) balls, approx 133m (145yd) per ball:
2 x balls each of:
104 Powder (pale pink) (A)
108 Lime (green) (B)
122 Violet (purple) (C)
105 Glacier (pale blue) (D)
103 Chick (yellow) (E)
115 Lipstick (bright pink) (F)
112 Prince (blue) (G)

4.5mm (US size 7) crochet hook

Yarn sewing needle

Finished measurement
Approx 17.5cm (7in) wide x 178cm (70in) long

Tension
Approx 5 bobbles across x 8 bobble rows over a 10cm (4in) square, using 4.5mm (US size 7) hook and Louisa Harding Cassia.

Abbreviations
approx approximately
ch chain
dc double crochet
rep repeat
RS right side
sp space
st(s) stitch(es)
tr treble
WS wrong side
yrh yarn round hook

Special abbreviation
5trCL (5 treble cluster): *yrh, insert hook in next st, yrh, pull yarn through, yrh, pull through 2 loops, rep from * 4 times more, yrh, pull yarn through all 6 loops on hook.

Scarf

Row 1 (WS): Using A, make 32ch, 1dc in second ch from hook, 1dc in each ch to end. (31sts)

Row 2 (RS): 1ch, 1dc in each st to end.

Begin bobble pattern:

Row 3 (WS): 1ch, *1dc in each of next 3 sts, 5trCL in next st; rep from * to last 3 sts, 1dc in each of last 3 sts. (7 bobbles)

Cut yarn, do not fasten off.

Row 4: Join in B, 1ch, *1dc in each of next 3 sts, 1dc in closing chain of next 5trCL; rep from * to last 3 sts, 1dc in each of last 3 sts.

Row 5: 1ch, 1dc in first st, 5trCL in next st, *1dc in each of next 3 sts, 5trCL in next st; rep from * to last st, 1dc in last st. (8 bobbles)

Cut yarn, do not fasten off.

Row 6: Join C, 1ch, 1dc in first st, *1dc in closing chain of 5trCL, 1dc in each of next 3 sts; rep from * to last 5trCL, 1dc in closing chain of last 5trCL, 1dc in last st.

Rep Rows 3–6, using colour sequence A, B, C, D, E, F and G and changing colour every two rows until scarf measures approx 178cm (70in), ending on a Row 6 and same colour as Row 1.

Last row: Rep Row 2.

Fasten off.

Finishing

Sew in ends.

Tip

When working a double crochet into the top of the 5 treble cluster, make the double crochet stitch into the closing chain at the top of the cluster.

Brighton rock
scarf

Materials
Debbie Bliss Angel, 76% super kid mohair/
24% silk lace weight
25g (⅞oz) balls, approx 200m (219yd) per ball:
3 x balls of 45 Hot Pink (pink)

4mm (US size G/6) crochet hook

Yarn sewing needle

Finished measurement
22.5cm (9in) wide x 227.5cm (91in) long (with
tassels)

Tension
Each square measures approx 10cm (4in),
using a 4mm (US size G/6) hook and Debbie
Bliss Angel.

Abbreviations
approx approximately
ch chain
ch sp chain space
dc double crochet
rep repeat
RS right side
sp space
ss slip stitch
st(s) stitch(es)
tr treble

Special abbreviation
2trCL (2 treble cluster): *yrh, insert hook in
next st/sp, yrh, pull yarn through, yrh, pull
through 2 loops, rep from * once more, yrh,
pull yarn through all 3 loops on hook.

Mohair isn't what it used to be, it's much softer! This stunning
scarf uses a lovely soft mix of mohair silk fibres. The squares
are made up of lots of chain spaces and are easy to make, but
it's important to practise the square first using a non-mohair
yarn, because if you make a mistake with mohair it's very difficult
to undo.

Squares
Working on RS of work throughout.
(*make 60*)

Make 5ch, join with ss to form a ring.

Round 1 (RS): 5ch (counts as 1tr, 2ch), [1tr, 2ch in ring] 7 times, join with
ss in third of first 5-ch. (8 ch sps)

Round 2: Ss in first ch sp, 1ch, 1dc in first ch sp, [5ch, 1dc in next ch sp]
7 times, 5ch, ss in first dc. (8 ch sps)

Round 3: Ss in first ch sp, 3ch, 1tr in same ch sp (counts as 2trCL), 5ch,
2trCL in same ch sp, [3ch, 1dc] in next ch sp, *[3ch, 2trCL, 5ch, 2trCL] in
next ch sp, [3ch, 1dc] in next ch sp; rep from * twice more, 3ch, join with
ss in top of first tr.

Round 4: Ss in first ch sp, 3ch, 1tr in same ch sp (counts as 2trCL), 5ch,
2trCL in same ch sp, *3ch, 1dc in next ch sp, 5ch, 1dc in next ch sp, 3ch,

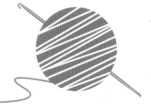

[2trCL, 5ch, 2trCL] in next ch sp; rep from * twice more, 3ch, 1dc in next ch sp, 5ch, 1dc in next ch sp, 3ch, join with ss in top of first tr.

Fasten off.

Tip

Sew in ends after making each square.

Finishing

Join squares in sets of three:

Place two squares with RS together and insert hook into corner 5-ch sp of both squares, *join yarn, 1ch, 1dc in same ch sp, [3ch, 1dc in next ch sp] 4 times.

Fasten off.

Open out squares. Place the third square on the second square with RS together; rep from * once more.

Fasten off.

Rep until all squares are joined, making 20 sets of three.

Join rows together:

Place two rows with RS together and insert hook into corner 5-ch sp of both rows, join yarn, 1ch, 1dc in same ch sp, [3ch, 1dc in next ch sp] 4 times.

*At the join make 2ch, 1dc in next ch sp (first ch sp of next square), [3ch, 1dc in next ch sp] 4 times; rep from * once more.

Fasten off.

Rep until all rows are joined, making 20 rows.

Make tassels

Cut about 240 strands, each approx 43cm (17in) long, and make each tassel with eight strands. Attach a tassel in each ch sp on the width edges (see page 27), so there are 15 tassels at each end.

sea view
scarf

I love this scarf. The yarn is really soft and even though it's a thick scarf it feels super cosy. I've used a self-patterning yarn, so the different colours emerge automatically from the ball without having to change yarns. The bright pink pompom gives it an extra zing.

Materials

Louisa Harding Amitola Grande, 80% wool/ 20% silk Aran yarn

100g (3½ oz) balls, approx 250m (273yd) per ball:

3 x balls of 123 Morgan (cream/green/blue) (MC)

Louisa Harding Cassia, 75% superwash merino/25% nylon DK yarn

50g (1¾oz) balls, approx. 133m (145yd) per ball:

1 x ball of 115 Lipstick (A)

5mm (US size H/8) crochet hook

Yarn sewing needle

Finished measurement

18cm (7in) wide x 220cm (88in) long

Tension

Approx 14 sts x 12 rows over a 10cm (4in) square using 5mm (US size H/8) hook, half trebles and Louisa Harding Amitola Grande.

Abbreviations

approx approximately
ch chain
cont continue
htr half treble
rep repeat
st(s) stitch(es)

Scarf

Row 1 (RS): Using MC, make a slip knot leaving a long tail for gathering later. Make 300ch, 1htr in third ch from hook, 1htr in each ch to end. (298 sts)

Row 2: 2ch, 1htr in each st to end. (298 sts)

Rep Row 2 until work measures approx 18cm (7in) finishing on a WS row.

Fasten off leaving a long tail (for gathering later).

Finishing

Sew in ends except long tail ends. Thread yarn sewing needle with tail of yarn from one end, make a running stitch along one end (of width), pull to gather and secure yarn at the starting end. This will gather the end into a semi-circular tube. Repeat on other end, making sure the gather pulls the same way as the first end, so the tube folds in the same direction, creating a wrong side and right side.

Pompoms

(make 2)

Using A, make 2 pompoms approx 7.5cm (3in) in diameter (see Cardboard Tube method on page 31), leaving long ends for securing to the end of the scarf.

Thread the pompom ends into yarn sewing needle and attach one to each end of scarf.

pavilion
scarf

Materials

Fyberspates Scrumptious DK, 55% merino wool/45% silk DK yarn
100g (3½oz) skeins, approx 220m (240yd) per skein:
3 x skeins of 105 Magenta

4mm (US size G/6) crochet hook

Yarn sewing needle

Finished measurement

Approx 20cm (8in) wide x 208cm (83in) long

Tension

Approx 18 sts x 16 rows over a 10cm (4in) square, working double crochet using a 4mm (US size G/6) hook and Fyberspates Scrumptious DK.

Abbreviations

approx approximately
ch chain
dc double crochet
dc2tog double crochet 2 stitches together
rep repeat
st(s) stitch(es)

Giant pompoms at the point of each end make a really swinging and fun scarf. It's made using a very simple double crochet stitch, with increases and decreases towards each point. The soft silk yarn makes this work really well. Use whatever method of making a pompom you're familiar with. I made mine using two cardboard tube inners from toilet rolls.

Scarf

Row 1: Make 4ch, 1dc in second ch from hook, 1dc in each of next 2 ch. (3 sts)

Row 2: 1ch, 1dc in each of next 3 sts. (3 sts)

Rep Row 2 for 45 rows or approx 25cm (10in).

Next row: 1ch, 2dc in first st, 1dc in next st, 2dc in last st. (5 sts)

Next row: 1ch, 1dc in each st to end. (5 sts)

Next row: 1ch, 2dc in first st, 1dc in each of next 3 sts, 2dc in last st. (7 sts)

Next row: 1ch, 1dc in each st to end. (7 sts)

Next row: 1ch, 2dc in first st, 1dc in each of next 5 sts, 2dc in last st. (9 sts)

Next row: 1ch, 1dc in each st to end. (9 sts)

Next row: 1ch, 2dc in first st, 1dc in each of next 7 sts, 2dc in last st. (11 sts)

Next row: 1ch, 1dc in each st to end. (11 sts)

Next row: 1ch, 2dc in first st, 1dc in each of next 9 sts, 2dc in last st. (13 sts)

Next 3 rows: 1ch, 1dc in each st to end. (13 sts)

Next row: 1ch, 2dc in first st, 1dc in each of next 11 sts, 2dc in last st. (15 sts)

Next 3 rows: 1ch, 1dc in each st to end. (15 sts)

Next row: 1ch, 2dc in first st, 1dc in each of next 13 sts, 2dc in last st. (17 sts)

Next 3 rows: 1ch, 1dc in each st to end. (17 sts)

Next row: 1ch, 2dc in first st, 1dc in each of next 15 sts, 2dc in last st. (19 sts)

Next row: 1ch, 1dc in each st to end. (19 sts)

Rep last 2 rows nine times more. (37 sts)

Next row: 1ch, 2dc in first st, 1dc in each of next 35 sts, 2dc in last st. (39 sts)

Next row: 1ch, 1dc in each st to end. (39 sts)

Rep last row for approx 117cm (46½in).

Next row: 1ch, dc2tog, 1dc in each of next 35 sts, dc2tog in last 2 sts. (37 sts)

Next row: 1ch, 1dc in each st to end. (37 sts)

Rep last 2 rows nine times more. (19 sts)

Next row: 1ch, dc2tog, 1dc in each of next 15 sts, dc2tog in last 2 sts. (17 sts)

Next 3 rows: 1ch, 1dc in each st to end. (17 sts)

Next row: 1ch, dc2tog, 1dc in each of next 13 sts, dc2tog in last 2 sts. (15 sts)

Next 3 rows: 1ch, 1dc in each st to end. (15 sts)

Next row: 1ch, dc2tog, 1dc in each of next 11 sts, dc2tog in last 2 sts. (13 sts)

Next 3 rows: 1ch, 1dc in each st to end. (13 sts)

Next row: 1ch, dc2tog, 1dc in each of next 9 sts, dc2tog in last 2 sts. (11 sts)

Next row: 1ch, 1dc in each st to end. (11 sts)

Next row: 1ch, dc2tog, 1dc in each of next 7 sts, dc2tog in last 2 sts. (9 sts)

Next row: 1ch, 1dc in each st to end. (9 sts)

Next row: 1ch, dc2tog, 1dc in each of next 5 sts, dc2tog in last 2 sts. (7 sts)

Next row: 1ch, 1dc in each st to end. (7 sts)

Next row: 1ch, dc2tog, 1dc in each of next 3 sts, dc2tog in last 2 sts. (5 sts)

Next row: 1ch, 1dc in each st to end. (5 sts)

Next row: 1ch, dc2tog, 1dc in next st, dc2tog in last 2 sts. (3 sts)

Rep last row for 25cm (10in), or to match first end.

Fasten off.

Finishing

Block and lightly press scarf with a damp cloth.

Make two large pompoms (see Cardboard Tube method on page 31).

Attach one pompom at each end of scarf.

Tip

When you are using this yarn, always wind skeins into a ball before crocheting.

Materials

Debbie Bliss Cashmerino Aran, 55% wool/
33% acrylic/12% cashmere 4 ply yarn
50g (1¾oz) balls, approx 90m (98yd) per ball:
3 x balls of 61 Jade (green) (MC)
2 x balls of 75 Citrus (lime) (A)

6mm (US size J/10) crochet hook

Yarn sewing needle

Finished measurement

Approx 19cm (7½in) wide x 187.5cm (75in) long
(without tassels)

Tension

Approx 14 sts x 16 rows over a 10cm (4in)
square, working double crochet using a
6mm (US size J/10) hook and Debbie Bliss
Cashmerino Aran.

Abbreviations

approx approximately
ch chain
dc double crochet
rep repeat
RS right side
st(s) stitch(es)
WS wrong side

cove
scarf

Sometimes it's the simplest that's the best. Double crochet is the shortest and easiest stitch and gives a tight texture, so I've used a larger-sized crochet hook on this scarf to give double crochet a looser and softer feel... and then there's the fantastic big tassel on the end.

Scarf

Row 1 (RS): Using MC, make 24ch, leaving a long end for making the gather later. 1dc in each ch to end. (23 sts)

Row 2: 1ch, 1dc in each st to end. (23 sts)

Rep Row 2 until work measures approx 187.5cm (75in), ending on WS and leaving a long tail for making a gather.

Fasten off.

Finishing

Sew in ends, except long tail ends. Thread yarn sewing needle with tail of yarn from one end, make a running stitch along one end (of width), pull to gather and secure yarn at the starting end. This will gather the end into a semi-circular tube. Repeat on other end, making sure the gather pulls the same way as the first end, so the tube folds in the same direction, creating a wrong side and right side.

Tassels

Make two large tassels (see page 28) – you will need nearly a whole ball for each tassel. If you'd prefer a smaller tassel, use less strands of yarn and make it shorter; the method is the same. Thread tassel ends into yarn sewing needle and attach one to each end of scarf.

anemone
scarf

Materials

Fyberspates Vivacious DK, 100% superwash
merino wool DK yarn

115g (4oz) skeins, approx 230m (253yd)
per skein:

1 x skein each of:

809 Peacock (dark blue) (A)

804 Sunshine (yellow) (B)

806 Sea Green (green) (C)

816 Crocus (purple) (D)

808 Blue Lagoon (blues/purples) (E)

811 Mixed Magenta (pink) (F)

814 Pebble Beach (grey) (G)

4mm (US size G/6) crochet hook

Yarn sewing needle

Finished measurement

Approx 7.5cm (3in) wide x 200cm (79in) long

Tension

Each flower measures approx 7.5cm (3in) in
diameter, using a 4mm (US size G/6) hook
and Fyberspates Vivacious DK.

Abbreviations

approx approximately

ch chain

cont continue

dc double crochet

dtr double treble

ss slip stitch

st(s) stitch(es)

Colourway

Make a total of 72 flowers using A, B, C, D, E,
F, G:

6 x A (dark blue)

11 x B (yellow)

6 x C (green)

12 x D (purple)

11 x E (blues/purples)

14 x F (pink)

12 x G (grey)

This is a really unusual and fun project – the flowers are sewn
together in groups of three, to form a lovely flower garland
around the neck.

Flower

(make 72, 10 each in A, C, D, E, G and 11 each in B, F)

Make 6ch, join with a ss to form a ring

Round 1: 1ch, 12dc in ring, join with ss in first dc. (12 sts)

Round 2: 1ch, 2dc in each st, join with ss in first dc. (24 sts)

Round 3: [3ch, miss 2 sts, ss in next st] 8 times. (8 loops)

Round 4: Ss in first loop, 3ch, 5dtr in same loop, 3ch, ss in same loop,
[ss in next loop, 3ch, 5dtr in same loop, 3ch, ss in same loop] 7 times.

Fasten off.

Finishing

*Take 3 flowers and put them on top of each other, placing the right sides
of the two outside flowers facing outward. Using a yarn sewing needle and
a coloured yarn from one of the outer flowers, sew the flowers together by
sewing around Round 2 of the flower (at the base of the petals). This forms a
3-flower group.

Rep from * until 24 groups have been made.

Join the flower groups together using the middle flowers only, by sewing each
tip of two adjoining petals of the middle flower to the corresponding petals of
the next flower group. Continue to sew flower groups together in this way until
all the groups are joined.

resources

UK STOCKISTS

Deramores
(yarn, crochet hooks, accessories)
0800 488 0708 or 01795 668144
www.deramores.com
customer.service@deramores.com

Designer Yarns
(distributor for Debbie Bliss yarns)
www.designeryarns.uk.com

Fyberspates Ltd
(yarn, crochet hooks)
01829 732525
fyberspates@btinternet.com
www.fyberspates.co.uk

John Lewis
(yarn, crochet hooks, accessories)
Stores nationwide
03456 049049 or 01698 545454
www.johnlewis.com

Love Knitting
(yarn, crochet hooks, accessories)
www.loveknitting.com

Tuition
Nicki Trench
Crochet Club, workshops,
accessories
www.nickitrench.com
nicki@nickitrench.com

Accessories
Addi Needles
(crochet hooks)
01529 240510
www.addineedles.co.uk
addineedles@yahoo.co.uk

Spellbound Bead Co
(beads)
01543 417650
www.spellboundbead.co.uk
sales@spellboundbead.co.uk

Knit Pro
(crochet hooks)
www.knitpro.eu

US STOCKISTS

Fyberspates USA
(See website for stockists)
www.fyberspatesusa.com

Knitting Fever
(Debbie Bliss,
Noro and Sirdar yarns)
Stores nationwide
www.knittingfever.com

The Knitting Garden
(Debbie Bliss, Noro and Sirdar yarns)
www.theknittinggarden.org

Webs

(yarn, crochet hooks, accessories, tuition)
75 Service Center Rd
Northampton, MA 01060
1-800-367-9327
www.yarn.com
customerservice@yarn.com

Accessories

A.C. Moore

(crochet hooks, accessories)
Online and east coast stores
1-888-226-6673
www.acmoore.com

Hobby Lobby

(crochet hooks, accessories)
Online and stores nationwide
1-800-888-0321
www.hobbylobby.com

Jo-Ann Fabric and Craft Store

(crochet hooks, accessories)
Stores nationwide
1-888-739-4120
www.joann.com

Michaels

(crochet hooks, beads)
Stores nationwide
1-800-642-4235
www.michaels.com

Unicorn Books and Crafts

(crochet hooks, accessories)
1-707-762-3362
www.unicornbooks.com
help@unicornbooks.com

Index

CROCHET STITCH CONVERSION CHART

Crochet stitches are worked in the same way in both the UK and the USA, but the stitch names are not the same and identical names are used for different stitches. Below is a list of the UK terms used in this book, and the equivalent US terms.

UK TERM	US TERM
double crochet (dc)	single crochet (sc)
half treble (htr)	half double crochet (hdc)
treble (tr)	double crochet (dc)
double treble (dtr)	treble (tr)
triple treble (trtr)	double treble (dtr)
quadruple treble (qtr)	triple treble (trtr)
tension	gauge
yarn round hook (yrh)	yarn over hook (yoh)

Acknowledgements

Books like this one are never a one-man show – it would be impossible to have achieved such a lovely collection of crochet scarves, in a beautifully produced book, without a very talented team around me.

My glorious crocheters were the usual suspects: Michelle Bull, Jane Czaja, Zara Poole and a lovely new addition to the crew, Lorraine Hurford. I am hugely indebted to them for crocheting so beautifully, patiently following my unchecked patterns and working to each deadline. Thank you so much.

CICO have, yet again, come up with a gorgeous looking book. My special thanks to Cindy Richards from CICO for commissioning me and also to Anna Galkina for just being lovely, super efficient and delightful.

There are also the people to thank who do tremendous work in the background on the pattern checking, editing, photography and styling. In particular I'd like to thank Jane Czaja, our pattern checker, who works super diligently and with a tremendous sense of attention to detail. Thanks also to Marie Clayton, who as always, did an exceptional job on the editing. Big thanks also to Sally Powell, art director at CICO, photographer Terry Benson, stylist Rob Merrett, illustrator Stephen Dew and to Vicky Rankin for the book design.

I've chosen my favourite yarns for this book and I'm very grateful to the suppliers who have been fantastically quick at getting the yarn out to me and the crocheters. Special thanks to Graeme Knowles at Designer Yarns and Jeni Hewlett at Fyberspates.

Big thanks also to my daughters, Camilla and Maddy, for being a great source of information and helping me keep the designs fashionable and current. Their honesty and sense of style definitely kept me on track. My thanks also to Victoria Solomon and JK for helping me get the non-creative bits in order at the beginning of the project, so that I could then be free to concentrate on producing the designs.